PLATE X

AFRICA.

EUROPE

Wild Boar
Lion

S. Limit of Camel
Elephant & Rhinoceros
Gorilla
Chimpanze

Hyena

ARABIA

Mecca
Suakin
Berber
Massowah
Khartoum

SOUDAN

NILE

Constantinople

Jerusalem

Hippopotamus

Giraffe

Heart of
Slave
Trade

MEDITERRANEAN

ALGIERS

Livingstone
died

Antelopes

Cagliari

Ustica
C. di Gallo
Gof Castellamare

C.S.Vito
Trapania
Favignano   Alcino

"Definite decision, as
'Ladies Beware!'"

E.A.WRIGHT BANK NOTE CO. PHILA.

THE TATTOOED MAP

Gibraltar

OCEA

Tangier
C. Spartel
Hindalia
Ceuta
Castillo so
C. Negro
C. Mazari
C. Tres Forcas
Cala Nuñ
Zera
Zaphra

Arzilla
R. Tetuan
Sahel
C. Viaa
Vagasca
C. Baba
C. Bocaya
C. Nuevo
C. Caladas

El Araiche
Alcantri
Pesadores
Penon
Al Buzema
Mehilla

Kasir Kabir
Al Kazar
Mostaza
Penon
R. Vacar
Resiffa
Zat

Mamora
El Kos
Rif
Garet

El Hoom
Wasen
L. Murja
Naranga
R. Etzagen
M. Teuzin
Carsis

Mehedia
R. Baht
Ruins
Hiaina
Temes
sun
Teve

Sallee
R. Seboo
Basra
Muley Idris
Z

Robat
Beni Meqquez
R. Leven
Alcass

Mansoria R.
Shella
FEZ
Teza
Cheik
Chaui

Sherudi R.
Massa
R. Beareg
Shulan
Dubbu

Dar al Beidur
Fidallah
R. Werra
Temure
Shelle
Soforo
Ougan al
Assan
Douboutou
Umer

Medina
Noukhaila
Guigo
R. Mahala
Tegar

Dela Roma
Al Krim
Morshana
Azarfa
El Guim
Berebers
Tezerg

Soubeit
Kaisar
Guer
El Eksebi
Beni Beseri

Marche
Terga
Adendoun
Tedla
Ain
Zeland
Kassabi
Shurefa
Kasir

Kella
Meshra
Halluf
Tamaroc
Zehbel
Mansor

Gherando
Tjijet
Morbeya R.
Maiat
Al Cala
Aebisak
Thurs
Tsalin
Gastir
R. Abou

Quassum
Tregegu
Tagodast
Evarae
R. Togdat
R. Ziz
Riv.

Smim
Shargna
Davara
R. Tafilet
Marca

MAROCCO
Biza
Afile
Kasr Abdal
lah
Segehnesa

Tasremoot
Bengali
Gourland
Kasr Maman

Miltsin
TAFILET

# THE

# TATTOOED

# MAP

BARBARA HODGSON

RAINCOAST BOOKS

*Vancouver*

First published in Canada in 1995 by
Raincoast Book Distribution Ltd.
8680 Cambie Street
Vancouver, B.C. V6P 6M9
(604) 323-7100

**Canadian Cataloguing in Publication Data**

Hodgson, Barbara, 1955-
The tattooed map

ISBN 1-895714-91-5

1. Title.
PS8565.O35T37 1995   C813'.54   C95-910404-6
PR9199.3.H62T37 1995

10  9  8  7  6  5  4  3  2

First published in the United States
in 1995 by Chronicle Books
275 Fifth Street
San Francisco, CA 94103

Book and cover design: Byzantium Books
Composition: Byzantium Books
Cover photograph: Barbara Hodgson

Printed in China

The author is grateful to the
following people for their
assistance with this book: my
acquaintances in Fes, M'hammedi
Alaoui M'hammed, for his Arabic
translation, and Berrada Abderrahman; Janine Giovannangeli,
for her help with the French
translations; and Karen Elizabeth
Gordon, Jeff Campbell, Andrea
Hirsh, Sarah Bolles, Karen Silver,
Nick Bantock, Annie Barrows,
and David Gay.

The maps of Tangier (facing page
24), Fes (facing page 44), Rabat
(page 53), and Marrakech (page
59) are reproduced with
permission from Hachette.
© Hachette 1948.

Maps on pages 16 and 17 appear
by permission of Rand McNally.
Map © 1943 by Rand McNally,
R.L. 95-S-201.

TO DAVID

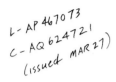

L - AP 467073
C - AQ 624721
(issued MAR 27)

HB. 902-856-58. 5/04
~~59~~ "
~~41~~ "
~~28~~ 3/04
~~29~~ 3/04
~~65~~ "
~~66~~ 16/4
~~07~~ "
~~08~~ "
~~61~~ 01/5
RC. 506. 743. ~~27~~ "
29
30
31
32
33
34
35
36
37
38
39

CAMPAGNE du MAROC

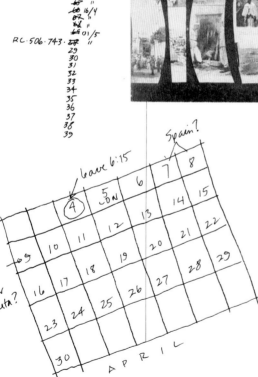

Spain?

leave 6:15

| | 5 SON | 6 | 7 | 8 |
| 4 | | | | |
| | | 12 | 13 | 14 | 15 |
| 9 | 10 | 11 | 19 | 20 | 21 | 22 |
| 16 | 17 | 18 | 26 | 27 | 28 | 29 |
| 23 | 24 | 25 | | | |
| 30 | | | | |

Morocco
Tangier or
Ceuta?

A P R I L

• Books (buy 1 more pbk for the plane)
• Cards (check full deck)
• Address book
• Money / traveler's checks
• Passports
• Toothpaste
• Alarm clock
• ~~Money~~
• Gluestick
• Spanish & Arabic phrasebooks
• Film - 120 & 35mm

April 4: The Plane

I am a traveler embarking on what I hope will be another success-
ful journey. I am not alone, but I doubt that my companion shares
my anticipation. We've traveled together many times before,
Christopher and I, and on every trip I've had the sensation that
the two of us have wandered—always together—to very different
places.

My travels inevitably begin with copious research and planning.
I began this kind of planning long ago when I was very young and
anxious to hit the road. Hours were spent poring over junior encyclopedias memorizing the names of exotic-sounding cities—Addis
Ababa, Samarkand, Damascus. Lengthy lists were written detailing
the most minute necessities: three pairs of socks, two pencils, spare
batteries, rope . . .

Looking back I can see that there have been no breaks from one
departure to the next; I start planning again before we've even
arrived back home. My life is constructed of destinations strung
together into one long flight. I love this travel—seeing, hearing,
smelling, touching something different every minute of every day.

I desire to learn everything there is to learn about the countries
we go to. Chris, on the other hand, simply arrives, somehow prepared, somehow interested, somehow knowledgeable, absorbing
our new surroundings but indifferent to detail. It must be this
assurance of his that attracted me to him in the first place. Now
it's sort of irritating because I suspect there's only luck behind it.
And, as for myself, I've started to dissect us in an attempt to see

Mrs. Connolly
(lady in 17c across
aisle)
68 Draycott Ave
Lдn sw3

| C | L |
|---|---|
| 4 | 8 |
| 16 | 12 |
| 20 | 16 |
| 34 | 22 |
| 40 | 27 |
| 42 | 35 |
| 48 | 41 |
| 54 | 45 |
| 60 | 52 |
| 72 | 60 |
| 89 | 64 |
| 91 | 70 |
| 94 | 78 |
| 100 | 85 |
| 110 | 92 |
| 114 | 94 |
| 120 | 102 |
| | 112 |

from magazine
left in the
departure
lounge.

seat nos. 17A & 17B
not bad spot except
squished!

Stewardess: Betsy Wilson
126 Duvernet, Toronto.
she knows C's aunt
Judith - remember to
pass along address.

the foundation to this—well—arrogance of his. When we started traveling together (it's been 11 years, imagine, over a decade) we seemed to be the perfect combination—hard work (mine) with graceful confidence (his). Although things have changed between us (and Chris would change them back if he had a chance), I think we are still perfect—if only because of our ability to spend hours in each other's company.

I talk endlessly to people we meet (having spent hours on foreign grammars learning how to count to 10 in dozens of languages); I ask for directions and for advice. Christopher, on the other hand, loathes speaking to strangers even in our own tongue—he derives pleasure in excluding contact with people from his experience of travel. I've given up questioning the way he acts and my behavior, whatever it happens to be, wouldn't make any difference to him. Anyway, we always find ourselves in countries upon which we both agree and where we both thrive.

Over the years we've developed a rhythm to traveling together. It is an understanding that shortcuts long discussions and has created a compatability that protects us like armor against people and events that might otherwise divide us. It's because of this that I know that neither of us would ever dream of traveling with anybody else.

I'm incredibly nervous, and I can't find the familiar consolation that writing in a journal so often provides. I usually keep a journal of sorts wherever we go. I persist in writing down departure times

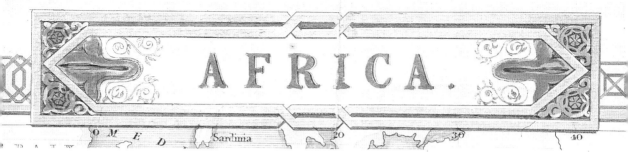

# AFRICA.

and flight numbers, important phone numbers, names and addresses, current costs, hotel room numbers, and restaurant menus. I write down the serial numbers of our traveler's checks and cross off the ones that we've spent, and I make a note of our passport numbers and issue dates in case the passports are lost—I know it's kind of dumb and kind of obsessive—but I value the memories that these trivial details recall. This time we are going to a new country with a strange and difficult language and alien customs. My reading has ill-prepared me for this new country itself: the accounts of the colonial conquerors and Victorian travelers along with the fiction and the poetry have left me with the conflicting senses of anticipation and ignorance. Perhaps this feeling is only the culmination of so many pleasant but uneventful trips to now-familiar places: France, England, the Caribbean, Greece. It's been a number of years since we've actually planned to go to an entirely new country. Whatever the cause, I find myself short of breath and giddy at just the idea of Morocco.

Christopher would never keep a journal, would never read a journal, mine or anyone else's. I long ago gave up trying to get

from same magazine — a reproduction of an old illustrated map

| C | L |
|---|---|
| 4 | 2 |
| 6 | 10 |
| 8 | 12 |
| 12 | 16 |
| 16 | 21 |
| 18 | 25 |
| 20 | 27 |
| 24 | 39 |
| 30 | 44 |
| 36 | 45 |
| 40 | 51 |
| 41 | 52 |
| 42 | 53 |
| 48 | 60 |
| 50 | 64 |
| 62 | 70 |
| 78 | 72 |
| 86 | 84 |
| 84 | 90 |
| 90 | 93 |
| 93 | 97 |
| 96 | 103 |
| 100 | 104 |
| | 110 |
| | 118 |
| | 124! |

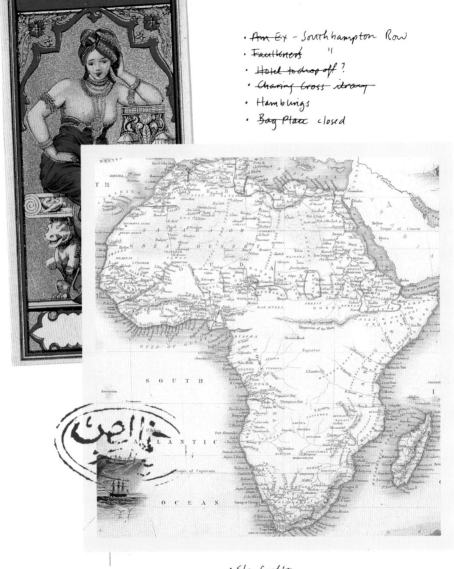

- ~~Am Ex~~ - Southhampton Row
- ~~Faulkners~~ "
- ~~Hotel to drop off~~ ?
- ~~Charing Cross library~~
- Hamblings
- ~~Bay Place~~ closed

- ~~Stanford's~~
- King's Rd / Dome  } next
- Pollock's           } time
- Gray's Market

him interested in travel accounts or guidebooks, but it's no use thinking that we would be lost without all my preparation. He is eternally prepared, with a sixth sense for arriving on time and paying fair prices. No, I plan only for myself.

He's that way with his business as well. He's lucky, Chris is, that he's able to work on these trips. People ask him to buy antiques for them when he travels. He saves up lists of desired furniture, fixtures, carpets, and so on, and then when we travel he just keeps his eye out for them. Spots something, buys it, sends it to the client, and manages to make a living doing this. Manages to make a good living. Very few people reject the things that he has picked out for them, and nobody has ever balked at the cost. I've come to see his assurance as arrogance; but others interpret it as a strong aesthetic sense. They trust him. I've rarely met his clients, to be honest; I lost the desire to after the first few. Stuck-up snobs. In fact we've hardly any friends in common.

I guess I'm lucky, too, with my research work. I know of no one else who can shut down on a moment's notice and take off for months at a time. We've tried to figure out how we could combine our jobs—him looking for things, me for ideas—but if you can't live together could you work together? I doubt it.

His apartment is lovely—filled with objects he couldn't bear to sell to anyone. My apartment is a shambles—filled with junk and ephemera that he turns up his nose at. But this difference, too, makes life interesting for both of us. For him, we sit in dark and fragrant antique shops drinking tea and conversing in low and

## IV.

### PREPARATIONS FOR "GOING OVER."

There may need to be another reminder following paper, like some of the others to ter it, is especially intended for those who h before crossed the Atlantic, and that, cons some of the advice tendered in it may seem B. C-ish" to those who have already taken the however low a one, in the academy of trav perience. To this the suggestion may pr added, that even some of those who have t degree may find themselves none the worse ing over these hints, even if they do so t from them. An apology may need to be n for the direct and conversational style ad this and some other papers; the aim of the in this regard to come as near as possib words and manner that would be used in conversation, with one of the parties doi more than half of the talking.

One word as to the mode in which w "wisdom" may be here contained—has been Or let the words be two, and embody them, mode of a late lamented dignitary, in a "litt Once upon a time, when the Shrewsbury rive Jersey, was more of a throughfare for p steamboats than it is to-day, a "hard c

*Roll #1 (ASA 100)*
*1-6: Vict; Alb. Fakes Room*
*7: Conran's Michelin Store*
*8-9: Italian Consulate*
*11-12: Taxi Cab.*
*Driver's name: Arnie Simpson*

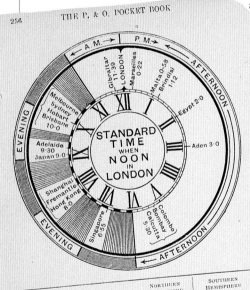

tasteful voices; for me, we scour the streets assembling a motley collection of sugar packets and menu cards, old bills and matchbooks. After all these years there's only one definite thing I know about Chris: he loves to search and it doesn't matter to him what he's looking for, even if it's my crummy old junk, and it doesn't matter to him if he finds anything. It doesn't matter to me either, and that's why he likes traveling with me.

Travel for us has few barriers. We carry passports from a neutral Western country; our religion, when we are required to write it on embarkation cards, offends no one. We travel with enough money to satisfy even the most disagreeable customs agents, and our plane tickets are never one-way.

Our itinerary, such as it is, is arranged only as far as Morocco. But we have six months off this time, so we may end up traveling across North Africa and back to Europe or we may end up staying in Morocco the whole time. Who else would plan a six-month trip without an itinerary? It really makes no difference—Chris has buying lists for any country in the world and I'm just happy to wander. If I had my way, I would wander forever and ever.

We should be landing in London around noon, and we hope to pick up a cheap bus fare to Spain in a day or two. Remind myself never to fly this airline again—what a crate. Can they possibly squeeze more seats in?

April 5, London:
Hotel—Rex Hotel near the British Mus.—it will be a relief to move south where it's cheaper. Glad to stay here though—it's given me a different outlook on London. Last trip it drizzled endlessly and never seemed to brighten from a dim sort of dawn-like gloom. We stayed in a basement room in an Earl's Court hotel. There weren't any curtains on the windows, so we hung up the sheets from one of the beds and slept tightly bound together in the remaining, monastically tiny bed. The hotel owner grudgingly supplied us with a tea cup (cracked) so we could brush our teeth but made us promise not to steal it. I was convinced that the best thing for London was another full-scale bombing. But that was last trip. Now the city seems alive and bright. I'd like to stay longer in case we don't get another chance on the way back—but we really must move south before it gets too hot.

April 6
We're booked on a fast bus to southern Spain. Leave tonight at 10 pm. It's cheap, about $52, and is due to arrive in Algeciras around 6 pm on April 8. There's a whole day ahead of us in the city. Chris has to go to some galleries to meet a couple of clients, and I'm

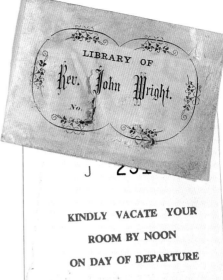

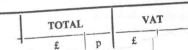

KINDLY VACATE YOUR
ROOM BY NOON
ON DAY OF DEPARTURE

....

| TOTAL | | VAT |
|---|---|---|
| £ | p | £ |

Rex Hotel:
Rm 22, 38 Bedford London
£ 38, single
£ 44, double
shower, etc. down the hall

Bus Europa:
Fare to Madrid £ 45 /
Fare to Algeciras £ 52 /
Leaves 10 pm at:
TOTTENHAM COURT Rd.
near Tube Stn.

BE THERE AT 9:30

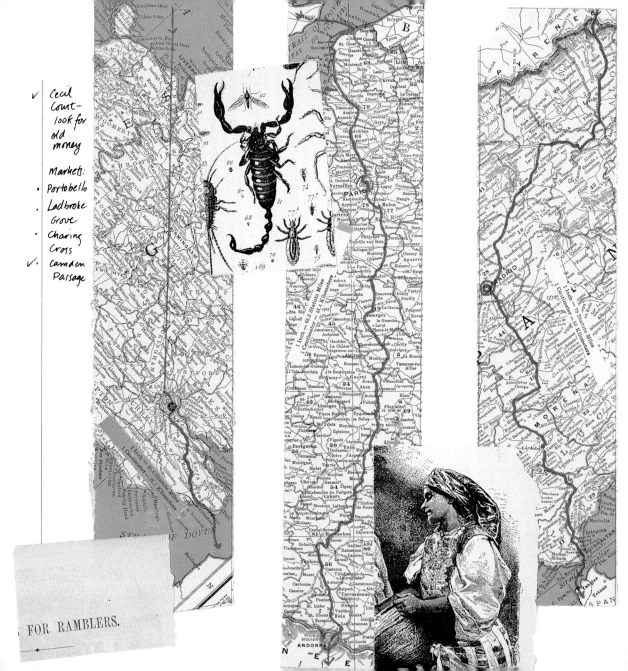

Cecil Court —
look for
old money

Markets:
- Portobello
- Ladbroke
  Grove
- Charing
  Cross
- Camden
  Passage

FOR RAMBLERS.

Marian & Lewis Pettigrew
22 Purns Court, Manchester M3 1142

DAMAGE NOTED

ROUTE TO SPAIN from LONDON

- Channel crossing - DARK (12:30am 'til 5:00)
- PARIS - dawnish not much traffic. Rain. Drove by the Eiffel Tower
- Toulouse - late lunch, overcast
- Through Andorra. Driver bought case of Pastis & perfume. Opened the pkg and made all us 'ladies' try some. What a stink!
- Zaragoza - too dark to tell what it's like
- 2am - Madrid. Can't see too well to write - we've hooked up with a taxi driver after circling the same streets looking for the hotel. No one said anything about paying for a hotel.

3am - found the hotel. Not enough room for everyone. We're going to stretch out on the bus to sleep.

BUS Driver: Marcel Conti: c/o Bus Europa 162 Tottenham ct. Rd. Get address from receipt and eggs for Gibraltar are almost always being embarked; the oxen are unceremoniously and cruelly swung on board by ropes attached to their horns. Here, as in the streets, every operation is accompanied by yelling and quarrelling.

The filthiness of the streets is a surprize even to the traveller who has just quitted Spain. The health of the inhabitants, nevertheless, is on the whole very satisfactory, thanks to the advantages of an almost unequalled climate. The prevalent winds all blow from the ocean, greatly alleviating the heat in the town and on the heights of the Marshan and Monte (p. 428) to the W. of it, and bringing frequent showers in the cool season (annual rainfall 36 inches). Snow and frost are almost unknown.

History. *Tingis*, probably one of the earliest settlements on the straits, ~~~~ in history until the Roman period. *Emp. Augustus* en-~~~ citizenship and *Claudius* made it a Roman colony. ~~~ 3rd cent. the territory of Tingis formed part ~~~ and under the constitution introduced ~~~ *Provincia Mauretania Tingitana.* ~~~itudes of S. Spain and

*Rereading*
*Gavin Maxwell:*
*Lords of the Atlas*

*Ferry ticket*
*1500 pts each, one way*
*3000 pts return, but*
*supposedly cheaper than*
*buying them in Tangier*
*- Bought one way tickets*

*• White wine - 42 pts*
*• Tapas :*
*Prawns (gambas) - 60 pts*
*Fried peppers - 50 pts*

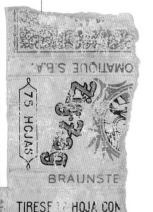

going to go to the travel bookshop on Long Acre and later on maybe catch a matinee—a couple of the plays look interesting.

April 8, Algeciras:
Arrived hours late and are staying at a dive near the harbor. We were in Algeciras about eight years ago—has this city ever changed. Huge apartment buildings line the shore road; the old center is being rejuvenated and the many vacant lots disorient me. The bars look the same but the servings of tapas are stingy and no one understands my requests for vino blanco—they keep serving sherry (fino blanco?) which is good and cold but too strong.

Bus trip was frankly horrible. It seemed to be dark for the entire trip—left at night and arrived at night—dark fog and rain through France. The driver got lost in Madrid, around 2 am, looking for a hotel that we were told we had to stay at. Either that or walk the streets for six hours. But by the time he found it (guided by a taxi driver) it was too late to put up there so we slept in the bus.

Sun and a café con leche at a roadside gas station near Cordoba.

April 9:
Nothing at all to keep us in Algeciras so we've got tickets for the ferry to Tangier. We were to leave at 1 pm but it is now 3 and the

only sign that we may leave eventually is the arrival of the Tangier boat and the disembarkation of its passengers. So many Moroccans. Why would I expect otherwise? From our line on this side of a glass wall we can see customs officials searching through their luggage. The line moves so slowly that I find myself speculating on their reasons for coming to Spain. My made-up stories have become so vivid that it's breaking my heart when someone gets turned back, and it's a personal victory when another is waved on through. And so many are turned back.

The last one is through now and three armed customs guards with rigid shoulders are going in to check the washrooms. I guess our line will start shuffling along soon. Chris sat down on the concrete floor (among all the cigarette butts), propped himself up against his pack, and promptly fell asleep. I won't wake him up till we really are moving. He slept on the plane, he slept all night at the hotel in London, he slept on the bus, he's sleeping now. He really is a wonder.

April 9, later:
Tangier. We've been surprised from the start. I had anticipated a reception like that described in the guidebooks, that is, one that would get you thinking about turning around and heading back to Spain. But hustlers and touts were so low-key that arrival was almost disappointingly anticlimactic.

We're in a rickety hotel on the square called the Petit Socco, right in the center of the old city, the medina. The room we've

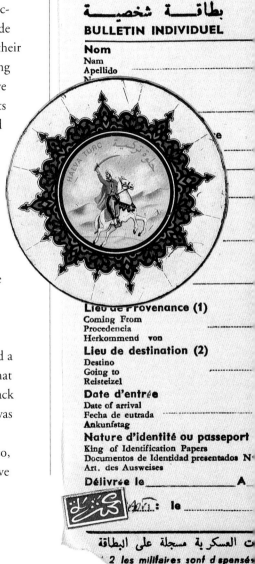

بطاقـــة شخصيــــة
**BULLETIN INDIVIDUEL**

**Nom**
Nam
Apellido
N

HALVA TURC

**Lieu de Provenance (1)**
Coming From
Procedencia
Herkommend von

**Lieu de destination (2)**
Destino
Going to
Reisteizel

**Date d'entrée**
Date of arrival
Fecha de eutrada
Ankunfstag

**Nature d'identité ou passeport**
King of Identification Papers
Documentos de Identidad presentados N
Art. des Ausweises

**Délivrée le** _____ **A**

الآرا .: le _____

ت العسكرية مسجلة على البطاقة
2 les militaires sont d spensé

MAROC

ICHA

been given, #14, is tiny and simply furnished with a painted plywood wardrobe, a wobbly table and chair, and a small double bed (the sheets are about six inches short of the end of the bed, revealing a lumpy, lurid mattress). The floor is covered with heavy clay tiles decorated in a repetitive geometric pattern. Some have loosened themselves over time so it's fun to walk back and forth across the room listening to the clunk, clunk of the tiles lifting and resettling as my weight dislodges them, one after the other.

I spent a few minutes pulling out the loosest ones to see if anyone was inspired enough to hide any contraband or secret messages, but alas, nothing. Nothing left in the dresser drawers or in the wardrobe either. A cigarette butt under the bed! Aside from the butt, the room itself is clean and fresh smelling and there's a lovely but warped set of French doors leading to a small balcony. I can imagine how cold this room would be in the winter; there's no heater and the door doesn't shut properly— the wind would whistle through without mercy. There are cracks in the windows and the space under the interior door, which leads to a drafty foyer, measures about two inches.

We don't face the square itself. We face a very narrow alley, and to step out onto the balcony is to invite yourself into the rooms of the hotel opposite. It is very cheap, I think, 112 dirhams, which is about $14.

#1.00 = 8 Dirhams

Send pic

Ahmed Abd es Salam
Hotel Kasba
15, place de Petit Socco
Tanger

Night:

I don't really know what to make of this city yet. Actually, it's not really a city but it's definitely not a town. The French word *ville* seems to say it the best. There's a mixture of lost sophistication—with the decaying, elegant homes and public buildings—and rawness, with the sounds of Arabic and the commotion in the streets. The thrill of trying to order a coffee in Arabic and continuing the conversation in broken French. Much more satisfying than France itself. The people here don't visibly scorn one's attempts.

Just sitting outside at a café—look up the name when we leave. There's an amazing tableau, seemingly arranged just for us. The shoe-shine boys cluster in corners together, every-once in a while darting out to approach a newcomer to the café. They do a rapid tap-tap-tap with their brushes against their boxes before pointing with the brush to the shoes, and then depending on whether they get a nod or a rebuff, they either get down to the business of shining the shoes or they retreat. The waiters come out now and then and shoo them away but no one else seems to mind them. The occasional beggar stops, sometimes alone, or if blind, with a guide. Men and boys form a constant parade selling everything: T-shirts, ladies' underwear, perfume, toys, pens, cigarettes, wallets (new), watches, pastries.

And foreigners: how easy it is to laugh at one's own when you sit back out of the light to watch. Silly hats (it's nighttime—why,

غرفــــة رقــم
Chambre Nº

الاسم العائلى

الاسم الشخصى

تاريخ ومكان الازدياد

SUCRE سكــر
POIDS NET 12 g.

قهوة
CAFES

Carrión

تاريخ الدخول

نوع اوراق التعريف او الجواز

سلمت فى
Signature امضـاء

1 و 2 يعفى العسكريون

Coffee: 3 DH
Orange juice: 7 DH

Coffee: qahwa

Qahwa
kehla-jooj
2 black
coffees

* Roll #2
1- Ahmed, hotel owner (send)
2- Hotel room, #14
3- View from room
4-5 Petit Socco
6-12 medina

*Café de la Paix*

oh why, do you need to wear a sunhat at night?), matching outfits (in case you forget who you're traveling with, you just look down at your own set of clothing to remind you?), grimaces, squints, grins, unease, indifference: the whole world passes by.

Every scene challenges reality. From the palm trees silhouetted against the sky to the fantasy, sugar-cube architecture framed by perfect vistas of the Mediterranean. Those lucky enough to be born here must sometimes—if they ever think about places like Canada—shake their heads at the thought of the dampness and cold and darkness of our world.

Every sense is on alert. My nostrils are sent out of control with each passing creature—human or animal—and at the turn of every corner or at the entry into every building another wave of odors hits. Jasmine and rose perfumes mix with garbage, the sea mingles with pungent vegetation, men wearing freshly laundered, sparkling white shirts jostle with others wearing never-laundered goat-hair cloaks. Faces are close—always—the hustlers, the store merchants, the taxi drivers. A collection of their breaths is storing itself into my nose's dictionary: the usual smells of garlic and tobacco, the unusual ones that still need translation.

We've been sitting in cafés all evening long and I catch myself staring at the impossibly good-looking men at other tables. C keeps having to snap me out of it. Embarrassing, really. Not that they aren't staring at us. Not that that's an excuse. But one man at one café in particular looked so suave, so knowing, so formal, as though he were a consul or a wealthy merchant. I stared at him and he stared back at me. And he looked so familiar as well—C thinks it's because he's following us from café to café.

The strange, discordant music—sometimes loud and jarring, more often soft and hypnotic—the warm evening air, and the dim, ineffective light from the kiosks and stores makes me feel that I'm on a set in a movie studio, but I'm neither acting nor directing, I'm watching the scenes.

April 10
So much for our hotel. I woke up with a tight cluster of flea bites on my left hand. Since we both react strongly, we've agreed to move to plusher accommodations. So off to the new city and fancier digs.

Established in a rather beautiful but run–down art deco-style hotel called the Martinique. We are paying the equivalent of $20 and have a bathroom attached to the room. There is a balcony here as well but this one looks out over the hillside descending to the beach. The combination of the breezes, which constantly keep the curtains in motion, and the cool floor tiles on bare feet moderate the temperatures and promise a refuge against the extremely warm spring sun. C is washing the clothes I had on yesterday hoping to rid them of any fleas I may be harboring. I hate doing laundry; I'd just as likely wear those clothes again as not.

Dinner
1 salad - 10 DH
2 chickens - 46 DH
2 Fantas - 8 DH
Tip        6 DH
          64 DH

Roll # 3 (100 ASA)        ✱
1- Hotel Stairs (5:30 pm)
2- View from hotel to sea
3- Room (# 202)
4- Hotel sign (art deco)
5-12- Bldgs along
        rue Pasteur

Now reading Lawrence
Durrell - Sebastian

miza - fruit from hotel
courtyard, looks like
an apricot

Trains to Fes - need to
change for all of them
  7:15
  9:30 ✱
  12:35
  3:05        ✱ very
                slow

flawless بِلا عَيْب . سَلِيم ٥ مُحْكَم

flax نَبات الكَتّان . قِنَّب . أَتْرَك

flaxen, flaxy كَتّانِيّ . شَبيه بالكَتّان

flax-seed بِزْرُ الكَتّان . شَهْدانِج

flay سَلَخَ . فَصَلَ الجِلْدَ عَن اللحْم

flea بُرْغُوث

flea-bane زَغْراء أَيُّوب (اسْمُ نَبات)

flea-bite قَرْصُ البَراغِيث ٥ فَرْصَةُ بُرْغُوث

flea-bitten مَدَنَّر ٥ مَرْقَط

fleam مِشْرَطُ أي رِيشَةُ فَصْد . لَيّل والمَواشِي

fleck أَرْقَطَ . ارقش || دَفِّش . طَ

fleshine

fleshless

fleshline

fleshly

flesh-me

fleshy

fletcher

fleur-de-

flew, of

From Durrell's
Sebastian !

"In cairo there is so much
confusion, noise, lights,
dust, fleas, people, daylight,
and darkness that nobody
who disappears is really
missed."

passion flower →
from courtyard.

Fortunately, some people have more sense. These flea bites are diminishing quite quickly but the area is just as red as when they were fresh this morning.

April 11:
The flea bites seem to have subsided. Although the area is still very itchy and very red, there are no bumps left at all. What is curious is that the red area seems to form a design of some sort. I pointed out the pattern to C, who only wants to know if I have any more bites. The cuff of my stiff cotton shirt brushes constantly against my skin and drives me up the wall. At least the dryness of the heat makes this clothing bearable.

Great luck! This habit of always checking out (snooping in) drawers and cupboards in hotel rooms has finally rewarded me with the jackpot: an old guidebook to Morocco—a 1943 *Guide Bleu*. I'll have to brush up my reading French to use it—but what a find! It's in perfect shape. Two satin ribbon page markers, beautiful, color fold-out maps. Delicately penciled-in notes in French in the margins. C's eyes are rolling. I know. What use is a 1943 guidebook?

Tangier is fascinating but we're having serious problems. We've been disagreeing on some fundamental issues, such as when to have meals and how to get to places. C says that the flea bites are making me pig-headed. They are driving me crazy: I reek of

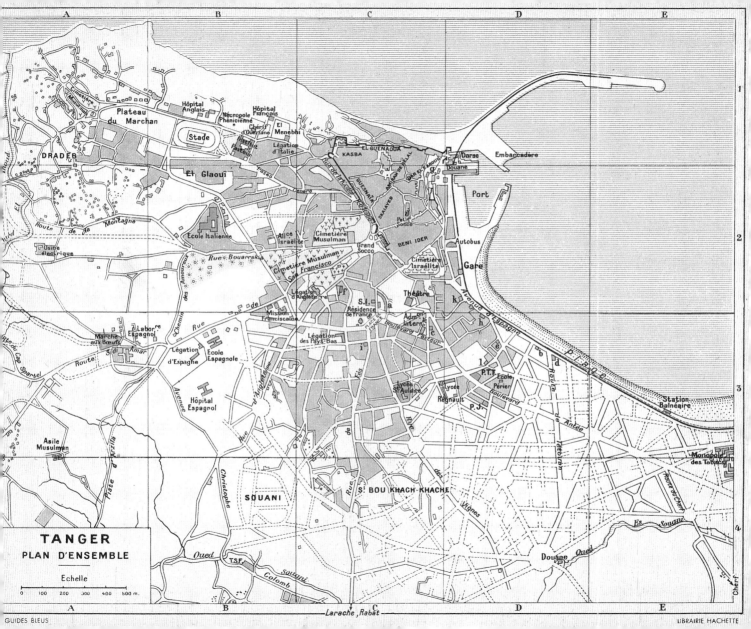

**TANGER**

PLAN D'ENSEMBLE

Echelle

0 100 200 300 400 500 m.

GUIDES BLEUS

LIBRAIRIE HACHETTE

Plateau du Marchan

Hôpital Anglais

Nécropole Phénicienne

Hôpital Français

Chenil d'Ouerrane

El Menebhi

Légation d'Italie

DRADEB

Stade

El Glaoui

EL GUENADUA

KASBA

Darse

Douane

Embarcadère

Port

Ecole Italienne

Usine électrique

Alice Israélite

Cimetière Musulman

Grand Socco

Petit Socco

BENI IDER

Autobus

Rue Bouarraka

Cimetière Musulman San Francisco

Cimetière Israélite

Gare

Légation d'Angleterre

S.I.

Théâtre

Laborse Espagnol

Marché aux Boeufs

Mission Franciscaine

Résidence de France

Adm. Intern.

Légation d'Espagne

Ecole Espagnole

Légation des Pays-Bas

Adm. Intern.

P.T.T.

Ecole Perier

Hôpital Espagnol

Lycée St-Aulaire

Lycée Regnault

P.J.

Station Balnéaire

Asile Musulman

SOUANI

Monopole des Tabacs

Christophe

T.S.F.

St BOU KHACH-KHACHE

Vignes

Douane

Oued

Es Souani

Colomb

Larache, Rabat

Route de la Montagne

Route du Cap Spartel

Piste d'Arzila

Avenue d'Espagne

Plage

Route de Tetouan

Route du Cherf

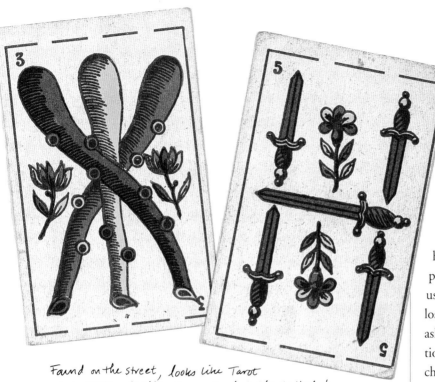

Found on the street, looks like Tarot but people play it. Find out what it's called & how it's played

musk oil and calamine lotion and irrationally sense that everyone who passes by knows that I have fleas.

I bought a map of Tangier but it doesn't help. C just puts it into his pocket and only pulls it out if I insist, usually miles after we're lost. Since C refuses to ask anybody for directions, I have to. Even if I check the map it doesn't seem to do any good. I get us hopelessly mixed up and turned around and end up taking us far out of our way. I do much better when it comes to retracing steps and finding places again. It isn't as though this is a

« فُـــنـــدق عـلـــي »

Roll #4 (100 ASA)
1- Anglican Church
2-5 - Cemetary
6- Walter Harris' grave
7- Church Keeper
8-12 Art deco bldgs.

Roll #1 - 35 mm
(100 ASA - Infrared)
had trouble with adapter
seems okay now
All 36 of hand except
about 5 wasted to
get things working

cream    burgundy

grey

Hotel room
tile

large place: Tangier is actually quite minuscule. But at any hesitation someone will come up and ask if help is needed, so we steadfastly and resolutely keep walking in hopes of not attracting too much attention. This morning a man asked us if we needed directions, so I asked if he could show us the way to the Boulevard Antée, a street name that I found on the Tangier map in the old *Guide Bleu*. The name changed around 1956, I guess, to Boulevard Mohammed V. The man who asked, an older fellow, thought for a few minutes then shook his head. I had the guidebook out so he leaned over to take a look at the map. Then he raised the book up to see its cover and started laughing, realizing that I was having a bit of fun with him. It was kind of like carrying newspapers from twenty years ago around, sitting down to read them at a café as if they had just been printed and then watching the face of the person who asks if they can borrow the paper from you, or like having old money that isn't accepted anymore and trying to pay for something with it.

Today I asked C why he travels. It had never before occurred to me to ask him. Either I took it for granted that we shared the same reasons (even though it's apparent that we do anything but) or else I was afraid of his reply. He answered that although some people he knew, including me, travel because of their infinite capacity to be interested, he traveled because of a desire for movement. I didn't comment—I want to think that over. But it strikes me as being a particularly honest statement.

April 12

This can't be the result of bites: it's a pattern, sort of like a kind of tattoo. I can't wash it off, and it is as red as the morning I woke up with it. The itchiness has subsided completely. I think I'll try photographing it and will stick the photo into the page opposite when we get home.

The man I saw at that café on the first night here has ended up at others that we've gone to. He does stare at me but it's a rather idle contemplation; I don't feel as though I'm on display, that I'm being looked over, as it were. It's more as though he thinks he knows me from somewhere. How I can tell that I couldn't possibly say. I really wouldn't have noticed him except he's so dignified that he seems out of place in these street cafés. He wears a three-piece suit of a very fine, brown material, must be wool. His shoes are beautifully polished and his hair and moustache are impeccably trimmed. His finely formed features exude an air of calm, and even the waiters, who yell boisterously at everyone else, speak quietly to this man. He occasionally pulls a photograph from his pocket and when not looking at me, studies this photograph. Do I flatter myself? I don't think so. There have been a couple of instances where I've almost felt that we were sitting at the same table, that we'd known each other for decades. Now I'm more positive than ever that I've seen him before. C rags me about falling for a mustache.

This constant scrutiny is unnerving. Normally, I would just walk over and confront the person. I've done that before and it usually embarrasses me, because, of course, the man you confront

Tangier street name change:

• Blvd Antée = Blvd Mohammed ✓

• rue des Vignes = rue Prince Heritier

• Passeo de Cenarro = rue du Dr. Cenatro

• rue de la Berrada = rue Sidi Bouabib

• rue del Monte = rue Arrakia

• rue Goya = rue Prince Moulay Abdellah

denies doing anything, but it stops most nonsense, eventually. Through the years, Chris has picked me out of the middle of a number of situations where I've taken men to task for whispering or staring, gesturing (that's the limit) or, oh yuck, even worse, hissing or tooth sucking. He doesn't have the endurance to wait and see who will win. I've gotten annoyed with him for interfering because he doesn't seem to realize that someone *has* to win.

Later:
I haven't dreamt at all since we've come here. Chris spends half of each morning telling me of his dreams, which is quite a novelty both for him and for me. He says he usually doesn't remember his dreams. I'm jealous; I miss my dreams and I told him so. He just grinned at me and said, "There's only room enough for one dreamer in these beds."

April 14
Somewhat behind in my rigorous record keeping. Visited the usual tourist stops, St. Andrews—a genuine Scottish church gently transported into Morocco by the addition of a few arabesque arches—Malcolm Forbes's villa and toy soldier museum, the Casbah palace with an infernally difficult-to-get-rid-of "official" guide. Later, generally wandered about photographing streamline buildings in the new city and the street scenes of the older section. We are planning to move on to Fes tomorrow. The weather is even more glorious than when we first arrived.

Roll #5 (100 ASA)
Infrared
1-12: Forbes Museum      *

Roll #6 (400 ASA)
1-3: Forbes Museum       *
4: Guard at museum
   (Soual) send pic
5-12: Wall around Kasbah       [send pic]

Guard at museum
Soual ben ~~Arba~~
            Aarba
Darb el Moussa #14
Tanger

Roll #2 - 35 mm (100 ASA)
Museum of the Sultan
(palace)   1-36

Roll #7 (400 ASA)
1-12 - Museum
medina - old city
suq or
souq or - market
souk

← Found at a stall in the street market just off the Grand Socco—Nothing else but old French novels and textbooks.

Marhaban - Hello
Ahlan wa sahlan - welcome
Salaam wa aleikum ) greeting
Alika Salaam )
Masa el Kher - good evening
Saba el Kher - good morning
Tcharafna - I'm honored

We passed by the first hotel we stayed at in the Petit Socco. The hotel owner, Ahmed, saw us as we walked by and came out to ask us why we moved if we had intended to remain in Tangier. How could I tell him that we thought his hotel had bugs? I told him that we had gone to the nearby town of Tetouan and that we were back just long enough to catch the train on to Fes. Do people believe travelers' lies? But showed him his address in my book, promised to send a copy of the picture I took of him and that if we came back to Tangier we would visit him even if we didn't stay. After saying goodbye, had to walk fast, which always draws attention, in order to catch up to C, who had wandered down the street during the conversation. The usual quantity of young men calling out, "Madame, your husband is here in my store. Madame!" Here, it appears, one is always watched and always assessed.

April 15

On the train to Fes. Talked to a young man in our carriage who had surrounded himself with notebooks and textbooks. I couldn't understand what he was studying but the course seemed to require a great deal of eclectic reading. He was quite a personable fellow, sort of good-looking, very at ease with himself, and intensely interested in our trip. We exchanged biscuits and fruit and I tried out a few of the rudimentary Arabic phrases I've been learning. The gratification one feels in response to the effort is phenomenal. I've had a number of satisfying conversations, and if the Western notion of friendship wasn't as austere as it is, I could say that I've already made a number of friends. The hospitality is generous here and sincere invitations to homes for dinner or tea are readily handed out. The trains are a surprise. I've heard it said that the railway officials will no longer sell third-class tickets to foreigners. So the days of the Marrakech Express appear to be over. Trains are comfortable and air-conditioned, have a constant stream of tea trolleys moving up and down the corridors, and are remarkably quiet.

Leaving Tangier was momentarily interesting, as the train ran for a ways along the port and then the beach. But we turned quickly inland and the views of the ocean were replaced by brown, dry, rolling hills; farmers' fields and laborers and the occasional scene of women and children washing clothing at ponds and streams. Most of the homes in the countryside are low, roughly built dwellings with multiple add-ons in all directions. A few swank places with crenellated walls around the house and yard.

Later:
We're in Fes, ensconced in a nondescript hotel in the new city.

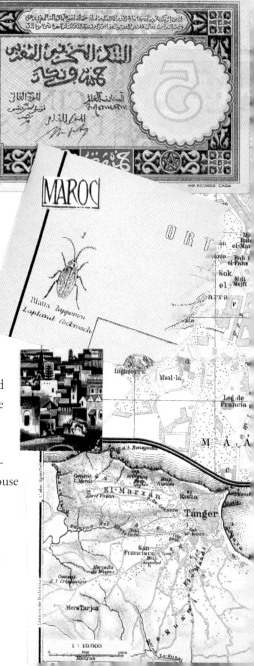

Roll # 8: 1-3 Tangier Port
4 - Compartment
5 - Mohammed
6-7 - Souk el Aarba -
everyone running
like crazy with
tons of baggage
changing trains

send pic

The train trip ended up quite merry. By the time we reached Fes we had a full carriage debating the Seven Wonders of the World and, more practically, which cities in Morocco merited our attention. The conversation, mainly between myself and the student and later with a young couple (with tons of bags) and an older gentleman with an impeccable French accent, was so lively that the time passed quickly. We were adopted by the couple, Mohan and Rabai, who walked with us at their great inconvenience, considering their pile of baggage, to the hotel we are in now.

Mohan's a polyglot, which describes his use of languages better than a word like multilingual. He doesn't distinguish between one language and another within the same conversation or even in the same sentence. Phrases like, "*Je vous en prie*, when you arrive in Fes, *faites attention* because, *Insha'allah*, there will not be a *problème!*" What problem he was imagining I am not sure. The conversation veered off in bizarre directions.

Rabai, who can speak only Arabic, kept interrupting by poking Mohan's side or pulling gently at his closest ear. She'd ask for interpretations or insist that he make her opinions or questions known to us. She asked us about families, divorce, marriage, children, in-laws, salaries. I was keenly aware of her fascination with me but she must also have been aware of my enchantment with her. She stared openly at me, so I met her gaze, smiled, and took the opportunity to search her face.

Rabai showed no hints of embarrassment or discomfort. She had an open and warm face that fluctuated between a sober

L'HIVER AUX PAYS DU SOLEIL

VÉRITABLE EXTRAIT DE VIANDE LIEBIG.

Mohammed Boutaib
24, rue Benalem
Tanger

expression bordering on impassivity and a wildly impossible grin. This sudden shift from one to the other without pauses at frowns or smiles or smirks got me thinking that she probably had one other expression worth watching out for—that of a virulent temper. After what must have been half a minute of this mutual face scouring we both burst out laughing. Rabai lunged over, grabbed my hands, declared we were sisters, and then told me that if I didn't want Chris around anymore, she knew someone who would. Mohan translated her Arabic into French and I, in turn, translated it into English for Chris, who made a feeble attempt at joviality. He bobbed his head up and down a couple of times, pulled the train schedule out of his pocket, studied it for a second, and then looked out the window. Everyone in the carriage was laughing at him, including me, I'm afraid.

I made further arrangements to visit Rabai and Mohan at their house in the old city, Fes el Bali. Not sure where that is because there are two old cities here, Fes el Bali and Fes el Djedid. But we are meeting Mohan tomorrow at one of the gates, and he will take us around the old cities and then to his house.

Mohan  Rabai

زبي شن

doesn't look
right (?)

Ayeet - tired
L'halshoun - it's hot
Ejma - take it away

6pm - Bab el
Ftouh

Taxis - Don't pay more than 10DH - except at night - 14 DH

Found this old pic
Hasn't changed except
fewer people are hanging
around now.
Mosque of Moulay Idriss
'mur des offrandes.

PRICE 4s.

4766

390

50

April 16

Spent yesterday evening and this morning combing Fes and becoming as familiar with it as possible for a newly arrived foreigner. Fes cannot be compared with any other place I have ever visited. One wishes fervently that change will never enter the city's gates; indeed it seems impossible that Westernization could ever be accepted. We've put all maps away for now. It's pointless. Street names are in Arabic and don't transliterate to correspond with any map. Efforts to stop and laboriously compare maps and street signs invites the rapt attention of bystanders. We find it far more enjoyable to simply put one foot in front of the other and to relish the prospect of being completely and deliriously lost. Lovely things have happened: Once we paused at a fork in the road and an old man came along and pointed confidently to one of them as if he was sure that he knew where we wanted to go. Once a child pulled me into a shop at the end of a dead-end street. Deaf to protestations, the child pulled and gestured "Come, come," and suddenly we found ourselves back on the street but not the same one; we'd been given the gift of a private shortcut.

The shops are fantastic. Teahouses are marked with little teapots above the door, dentist offices with crudely painted signs of smiling mouths and big teeth, not to mention delectable window displays of dentures and gold fillings. Medicinal shops are festooned with wizened animal pelts, embalmed mice and rat

· craya - difficult
· kalyptus - eucalyptus

corpses, and reptile skins. Bushels of dried grasses and leaves are surrounded by bulging baskets of herbs and colorful spices. Patterns for decorating hands with henna, boxes with beauty formula, small sachets in flourescent greens and pinks, packets of tea, insect repellents, and hand soaps are all mixed in together.

Garlands of dried figs embellish the awnings of the date shops. As we pass by, the merchants whip out irresistible samples of their finest dates. My shoulder bag is now full of small packages of dates, apricot preserves, figs, almonds. More easily resisted are the olive sellers, not because their products aren't as enticing but because the logistics of carrying bags of olives around just don't work. I pause often in these sections, breathing deep the warm, comfortable scents of oils and spices and studying the multi-colored jars filled to their brims with pickled eggplants, radishes, peppers, and olives. At night these shops are particularly mar-velous as the colors take on an even richer life under the light of the bare, incandescent bulbs.

## Casablanca de 1889 à nos jours

Album format 25 × 32
× 18, tirées en héliogravure
J.-M. GOULVEN,
avocat au barreau de Casablanca

Mettant en regard dans chaque page d'illustration une rue ou un quartier de Casablanca tel qu'il était autrefois et la même vue telle qu'elle est actuellement.

Ces Photos rigoureusement authentiques, font de cet album un document précieux et vraiment intéressant pour tous.

PRIX : 5(

Editions " MARS ", 128, rue

Rolls 9 – 14 (400 ASA)  *
Fes – who knows which
streets – I give up!

fondouk ⎱ market
    or ⎰ place and
fondouq    hostelry like
           a
           caravanserai

← Found great old store on trek with Chris
lots of pics.

Merchants sit on divans at the entrances to their shops and call out to passersby. More often than not the calls are to greet friends rather than to make sales.

Around every corner is a feast for the eye and the ear—the frozen surprise of children not expecting a lost foreigner in their quarter, the play of dust caught in a chance ray of sunlight, the gurgle of water and laughter at a public fountain.

We met Mohan at Bab Ftouh, one of the gates to Fes el Bali, far from the hustlers who congregate around the main gates. He led us through twisting streets, down alleyways reeking of rotting vegetables, through markets, past narrow doorways of houses and shops. His home is a small, dank apartment on a very poor street, but the inside is furnished comfortably and his two children were dressed very well. We were greeted with great affection by Rabai and served quantities of coffee, oranges, and cakes. C was accepting the attention that such a visit generates but I could tell that this was uncomfortable for him. Future visits, I think, I will make on my own.

I asked them if they would like me to take some pictures of them so we all trooped up to the roof and I took photos of everyone (I got the feeling they were doing this more to please me than to please

Mohan & Rabai
(Children are Ajroui
(Ajraoui?) and Mohammed)
Oued Souaffine
Derb ben Arsa
Nº 37 - Fes

send pics

✳ Roll #15 (400 ASA)
· Family, roof top, etc.

themselves). The pictures will look pretty crazy with the backdrop of madly patterned sheets and blankets whipping about on the lines and in the distance the frenzied convulsion of roof lines, neighbor's laundry, and television antennas. I've taken photos of the family and some neighbor's kids and have promised to send them.

April 17

Last night after we had turned out the lights and I was just about asleep, Chris sneezed twice—quite loudly. A voice from the room next door said, "*El hamdulilah,*" Arabic for "Bless you." It sounded like someone else was right in our room. Chris replied, "Thank you," in an absentminded way, as if he thought I had said it, and the voice answered with a heavily accented, "You're welcome." I stretched my hand out to touch the common wall just at the head of the bed, expecting to feel something gauzy and penetrable instead of the wood and plaster and paper of the wall. For what other substance would transmit such sounds rather than barricade them from us? My fingertips ran over the ribbed pattern of the paper and I imagined the person next door sitting next to the wall, sharing the same darkness and tracing the movement of my hand while waiting for another sound to respond to.

C has gone off for the day with a university friend now working in Fes. They want me to meet them this afternoon for coffee at a café I haven't been to. I must stick the note he left for me in here—it makes no sense to me whatsoever:

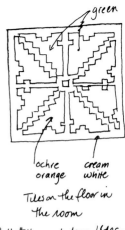

green

ochre
orange

cream
white

Tiles on the floor in
the room

Roll #16 - art deco bldgs.
new city ( 100 ASA )

Cafeteria

LYDIA: WHY DON'T YOU
MEET US AT THE CAFE
I TOLD YOU ABOUT
YESTERDAY? IT'S
BEHIND RUE MOHAMMED
V ON THE ST. 2 BLOCKS
SOUTH. SEE YOU AROUND
4. Christn

Never is the café's name mentioned. Boulevard Mohammed V is quite long and none of the other parallel streets could be described as any number of blocks south—the street runs practically north/south. I'll go out later and look.

April 17/10:30pm
Where do I start? The most unbelievable thing has happened. I'm back at the hotel—alone—after a lengthy tour of cafés on both sides of Mohammed V. There weren't that many but they were spread really far apart. I stopped in for a coffee at the Café Metropol—it's just down from the Grand Hotel—and I ran into the man I noticed in Tangier, and I spoke with him. Apparently he owns this café, the Metropol, which doesn't explain my impression of his sophistication. However, when we started talking, inevitably since we both recognized each other from Tangier, my first response was not diminished but rather reinforced. He came over to my table and must have stood there for a minute before I noticed him, since I had been gazing out of the window. I invited him to join me. As he sat down, I introduced myself and offered my hand to shake. He politely dismissed the extended hand, but

before I could decide who had offended whom he took my left hand in his and started to raise the cuff concealing the tattoo. I must have blushed a deep red—this was particularly unnerving—but I didn't think to withdraw my hand. It was helplessly cradled.

He spoke to me in a mixture of English and French as he examined the pattern, tracing its form with his clean and rather feminine fingernails, and as he spoke, the air in the café seemed to change, becoming denser. The other patrons began to fade away and yet the talk around kept growing louder and louder, surrounding us in a cocoon of noise. He unravelled a story, slowly, like a reluctant insomnia. The steady, monotonous voice so much like my own thoughts—repetitious, relentless, unforgiving. I panicked as his finger traced round and round the tender skin of my wrist and tried to pull my hand away. His grip tightened and I heard him say, "Only your skin and your tears will allow you this journey." He finally released my hand and carefully, gently pulled the cloth back over the wrist. And then he placed his own left hand, fingers splayed, on the tabletop. With the tips of his thumb and index finger of his right hand he raised his own cuff, revealing similar markings. I could feel the blood pounding in my ears, and I fought the instinct to touch his skin. As he pulled down his shirt sleeve, the air cleared, the conversations around us resumed a normal pitch. I wanted to ask him about the map tattooed onto his arm but I felt as though I'd already been told and that, although it was very important, I didn't or couldn't yet understand it.

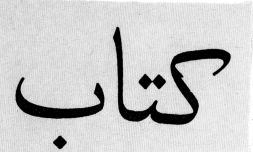

كتاب

Layash Boussalem
boulevarde du Quatrième
Tirailleurs , #15
Fes
(near Grand Hotel)
—————
check prices at Grand Hotel
—————

He went on to tell me about Morocco and Arabic and Islam. His name is Layesh, and he described himself as a hadj, which is a Moslem who has made the pilgrimage to Mecca. The word comes from hejira, or flight, a word I have come across often in my reading, a beautiful word that seems to describe my travels, although pilgrimage seems to be too significant a word to use in translation. Flight—seems evasive. Just plain departure suits me better. I asked him when his pilgrimage had been and if he ever traveled outside of Morocco now. He replied quite vaguely that he had gone a long time ago and then he sat forward suddenly and declared he would never stop traveling.

He asked me about my travels. Well that's like saying to someone, "Tell me about your life." So I just said that like him I always traveled and if I had my way I, too, would never stop. He smiled and told me that I was one of the rare people, someone who could possibly understand his life. The conversation was too surreal to interpret the remark as a gambit, but writing this out now it sounds foolish.

I had him write down his name and address for me. We've not made arrangements to meet again as it seems so certain anyway. We shook hands; he waved away my attempt to pay for my coffee; I smiled as I said good-bye and left the café. How could such an encounter end so ordinarily?

№ 090051•

5.00 DH
خمسة دراهم
cinq dirhams
Cinco Dh

اقتيم
TAXES

Purice | Flea | برغوث
بوليس | فلي |

Pulga | Floh | Puce
بولغا | فلوه | بيس

April 17—11:00 pm
Still alone, checked reception, no message—what are they up to?

Midnight
Checked reception, again—no message. The clerk definitely feels sorry for me.

April 18:
*Got back at 12:30. Allen and I waited at the café for three hours before going for dinner. Well—not just waiting but catching up on old times.*

*I can't bring myself to ask how you could have missed us—we sat at the front of the café next to a large picture window. Glancing at my note, I can see why you might have had a little trouble, but were you really looking?*

*I still don't know the name of the café, but I'll take you there today and buy you a coffee and a sweet. How do you like the tea label?*

April 18
Get your own book.

Roll #17 (100 ASA)
1-12 — more bldgs, new city

Café Stella
- coffee – 5 DH
- cakes, western style – 7 DH
- orange juice – 7 DH

Café Metropol
- coffee – 3 DH

- Reception clerk:
Menhabi Rachidi
c/o Hôtel Cecil
rue du Soudan, 80
Fes

Bagra – cow
Howli – sheep
Sachman – donkey
Labnel – horse
Berrarej – stork

Fes - tiles, ceramics, roof tiles
(olive pits to heat kilns)
Blue = Fes
Green = North
Brown = Safi

C and I returned to his café. Strange, but it was the Café Metropol where I had spoken at length with Layesh. I must have arrived there just after they left. How often does it happen that people wait for each other in the same place but miss by minutes?

There was a man there who recognized C and welcomed us both. He asked if I was the friend they had looked for yesterday. When told I was, he laughed and asked me how it was possible that I had missed the most popular café in Fes. I told him I had actually come here yesterday, probably after Chris and Allen had left, and had asked about the two, had a coffee, and talked to the owner. He told me that was impossible: he was the owner, and furthermore, he had been at the café for the entire afternoon and evening and had not seen me. I insisted, after all, I *was* here. Everybody looked at me as if I was crazy. And C—honestly, you'd think he would back me up once in awhile. Instead he poked me in the side trying to get me to shut up. But if Layesh isn't the manager of the café like he said he was did he also lie to me about his address? He's told me something that has stuck like a dream I can't remember and I need to see him, to ask him to repeat what he said. I haven't allowed myself to think about this as it seems so absurd. I'll be leaving Fes soon. How can I get in touch with him if he's been lying to me? I saw that the conversation was becoming uncomfortable, so I let up and admitted to being mistaken. We all relaxed and C and I sat down and had some coffee and cake. The owner came by again later and formally introduced himself to me (Chris had forgotten his name and isn't much for introductions anyway). He told me his name is Abderrahman and that this cafe has been in his family's possession for seventy years. I asked him if he had any menus or bills from way back but he misunderstood and had a waiter bring out a new menu for me.

We talked to a couple of people who passed by, people C had been introduced to yesterday afternoon when there with Allen.

Allen came in later on and sat with us. I met him years ago when we were both hideously adolescent. He still is. No, that's not fair; he just hasn't figured out that he doesn't need to impress us with his academic credentials. I keep trying to think of his good side but his heavy glasses and short-sleeve shirts, with sleeves that are too short, keep getting in the way. And you can see his undershirt through the shirt material (it's probably polyester), and he keeps his wallet

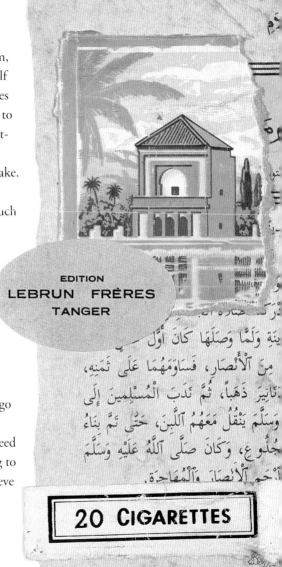

EDITION
LEBRUN FRÈRES
TANGER

20 CIGARETTES

in his back pocket and it drags down his pants, which are too loose. There, I've written it down, now I can relax and continue trying to think about his good side. He's here, for a start, and not in some stuffy department in some backwater university. He's enthusiastic about North Africa, has advanced a fair way with Arabic, and doesn't complain about anything. To be perfectly honest, his description of life in Fes was fascinating and I envy him for the intimate knowledge he'll have by the time he leaves. I suggested to Chris that we could consider staying in Fes for an extended time and perhaps take some Arabic lessons, but of course he's not enthusiastic. This is a hard city—noisy, dirty, and crowded—but there is so much life I could actually stay here in spite of the drawbacks. However, we plan our onward itinerary with gusto.

Allen, who has traveled considerably in this area, has helped a lot with our plans. But it is up to us to decide whether to head to Algeria and Tunisia after Morocco or to head back to Spain and east to Greece.

April 20, still Fes
Spent yesterday and part of today with my ancient *Guide Bleu* attempting to retrace some

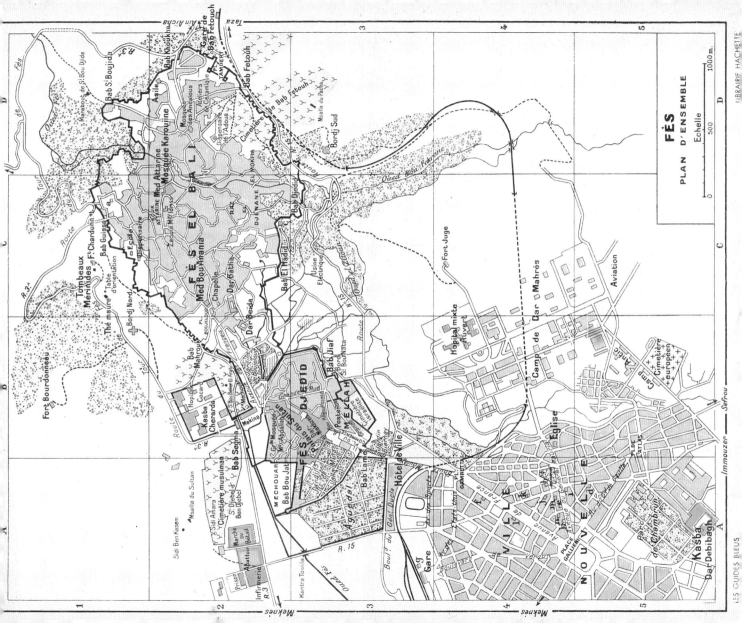

FÈS

PLAN D'ENSEMBLE

Échelle

0   500   1000 m.

LIBRAIRIE HACHETTE

FÈS EL BALI

Mosquée Karouiine

Med Attarine

Med Bou-Anania

Tombeaux Mérinides

Fort Bourdonneau

FÈS DJEDID

MECHOUAR

MELLAH

Camp de Dar Mahrès

Aviation

Hôpital mixte

Fort Juge

NOUVELLE VILLE

Kasba de Chambrun

Kasba Dar Debibagh

Gare

LES GUIDES BLEUS

Blvd de Verdun =
Blvd Tariq Ibn Ziad

Fes -
. Avenue de France =
    Ave. Hassan II

. Avenue du Général Maurial =
    Ave. Mohammed Slaoui

. Ave. du Général de Gaulle =
    Ave. Youssef ben Tachfine

. Ave. Foch =
    rue Mohammed el Hansali

. Blvd du Quatrième Tirrailleurs =
    Blvd Abdallah Chefchaouni

. Place Gambetta =
    Pl. de la Résistance

of the areas on my own, especially in the new city. Most of the streets and alleys remain unmarked in the mazes of the two older sections, where the mapmakers seem to have given up in despair. But it's fairly simple to follow the main routes. I tried repeating the exercise with C in tow one evening but streets that I easily identified on my own I just couldn't find again. The Café Metropol is on a street that used to be called the Boulevard du Quatrième Tirailleurs. No wonder they changed the name, it's so cumbersome—The Street of the Fourth Snipers, Fourth Freelancers. It must refer to a French military division. The Café Metropol isn't mentioned in the book; there's just a passing reference that on this particular street one can find many cafés and restaurants. Hold it, Boulevard du Quatrième Tirailleurs is the name of the street on Layesh's address. He wrote down the old address of the café, not a home address. Why on earth would he do that? I've got to see him again.

April 21
Either the young hustlers have started to recognize us or we are getting slyer in our movements. Whichever, we now walk unhindered through all sections of the city. Chris's purchases list has

FOR ATTRACTIVITY AND BEAUTY

Rolls #18 & #19
· medersa bou Inania
· Street scenes, old city
  Fes el Bali

Roll #20
· The Mellah - the old
  jewish quarter
  Fes el Djedid

* (ASA 400) *

وان لم تحضر في وقت
السفر لاتقبل منك شكاية
Aucune réclamation n'est
admise des voyageurs man-
quant Le Départ

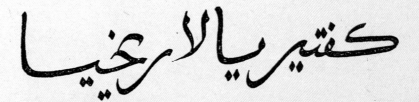

كفتي يالارخيا

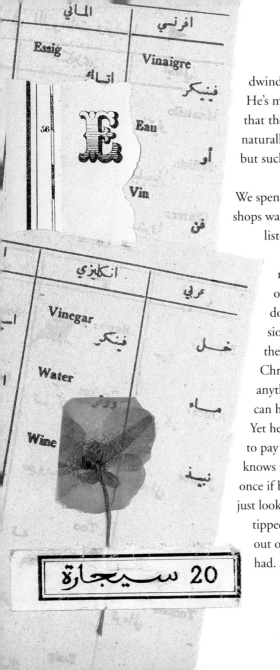

dwindled quickly here as there are literally hundreds of shops. He's made so many trips to the post office to send things back that the post-office clerk invited him home for dinner. Chris naturally declined—politely as ever. I wanted to accept for us but such interference would never have done.

We spend a lot of time together sitting quietly in musty carpet shops watching rug after rug being swept out in front of us and listening to the murmurs of persuasion. I watch Chris during these moments when he's dealing with the merchants. He doesn't bargain. He doesn't make any offers. I don't think he's ever even said so much as "What does it cost?" He just sits there with absolutely no expression on his face and the merchants start with a price and then just drop it and drop it and then drop it again until Chris says, "Okay, I'll take it." He hasn't bothered to learn anything of Arabic, not even a few polite salutations, and he can hardly speak any French although he understands some. Yet he knows instinctively what to pay the tea man and what to pay the man who bundles up the purchases. That he even knows that these people are to be paid amazes me. I asked him once if he'd read up on tipping and bargaining protocol, and he just looked at me like I was too naïve for words. I asked him if he tipped the post-office clerk to make sure that the packages got out of the country. He acted offended and then admitted he had. And then, a little while later, he started bragging about

how he got away with tipping the clerk some ridiculously minis-
cule amount. I say, wait and see if the parcels arrive. We're both
cheap but he takes the cake.

We also spend a lot of time walking in the heat aimlessly. Our
differences are softened as we stroll without question towards
cafés, no longer standing outside discussing—"shall we?" "shall we
wait?" "you go first" "you decide" "shall we try somewhere else?"
The cafés draw us in with more than the promise of a cold drink
and a shady terrace or air-conditioned salon—we've become part
of the city and need to watch it pass by. The noises are now
accepted as bearable, the odors welcome sensory signals, the glare

SCENES
et
TYPES

PIESSE & LUBIN
ENGLISH
PERFUMES
KISS-ME-QUICK
Ce parfum delicieux, exquis, est en-
tièrement different des odeurs connues.
OPOPONAX
Se trouve chez tous Parfumeurs
Droguistes et Maisons Anglais
LONDON
2 NEW BOND STREET

of the sun off the streets and buildings a necessary part of the
dream. A dream it is, as we would never belong here no matter
how welcome we were made to feel. So it's time to move on before
delusion takes over completely.

   Have spent several evenings and one entire day with Mohan
and Rabai. Except for the first visit I've left Chris back at the

Bajaddoub باحروب            باحروب
                   b-u-d-j-b
        باحروب

silu – سلو

(kind of a Moroccan
trail mix)

ingredients: mix together –
almonds, wheat, sesame,
farine, tahina, mastic,
neva (?) – green seed –
how helpful, oil,
cinnamon

$1 kg$ Tehin $+ \frac{1}{4}$ beurre
$+ \frac{1}{4}$ huile

⎰ Mohan's explicit
   directions!

(what is the difference
between farine and
wheat?)

Rachel Guillemot
(friend of Allen's)
79, rue du Commerce
Fes.

---

hotel and have made excuses. With their help, my knowledge of Fes, although far from complete, grows every day. The red pattern stays pretty much hidden by the cuff of my sleeve, and I keep it that way to avoid discussion. I've helped in the kitchen squeezing oranges and slicing vegetables, hung out on the roof with the children, and gone out of my way to avoid a visit to the hamman— the local bath—where I'd have no choice but to expose my wrist. It's getting dicey though; Rabai keeps insisting.

We leave for the capital, Rabat, tomorrow via Meknes, where we will stop for a day or two. Because we have finally decided to travel to Tunisia after leaving Morocco (C's preference), we intend see if we need to arrange for Tunisian visas in Rabat.

Buses to Meknes leave constantly—the trip is only an hour or so but as a farewell gift Allen has arranged for a taxi and driver to take us there via the Roman site of Volubilis. Apparently there are very few such remains in Morocco and Volubilis is the best of them, with a superb collection of mosaics, most still intact and in place. It's a miracle that Allen made these arrangements; yesterday I had been in despair studying the guidebook's suggestions for getting to Volubilis *sans* car. For those of us too cheap to hire a taxi for the entire trip, the route involved a Fes city bus or taxi to the outskirts, a half hour to hour wait for the local bus. A ride on that bus to a junction. Then a two or three km walk or hitchhike to the site itself. It's apparently easier to get there from Meknes but I have a horror of backtracking. Allen warns us not to pay any extra once we reach Meknes and to insist on being dropped off at the hotel of our choice. The driver, Mohammed, apparently has family in Meknes as well as in Fes so a one-way fare is no problem for him.

April 22

Left Fes around 7:30 am in order to beat the heat at Volubulis. We circled the walls before climbing up beyond the city past rolling fields cultivated into tiny, perfect patches of deep and light greens alternating with yellows and browns. We drove through small market towns with long lines of slow-moving, overloaded trucks and carts fanning out in both directions. Precarious loads of huge, purple Spanish onions or brilliant green and yellow melons caught the eye and presented a falsely comforting picture of abundance. Our taxi, a Mercedes-Benz that Mohammed dusted and polished at any opportunity, passed the market convoys easily.

We were the first people at the site, arriving at 8:30. Mohammed took us around but his interest was limited to arriving in Meknes as soon as possible. We lingered against his will, steadfastly searching out the famed mosaics, but gave up when it became too hot.

He detoured to the holy town of Moulay Idriss, named after a saint. It's so sacred that non-Muslims are not allowed to stay the night there. Mohammed himself would not stop in it, but not for reasons of sanctity and respect. He skirted the town while spewing pejoratives towards the inhabitants—*"Voleurs! Assassins! Drogués!"*—

Roll #21
Volubulis : roman gate
   - mosaics
   - Driver -
      Mohammed
      ~~Mbrouti~~
      Mbrouki

Roll #22 (ASA 400)
1-4 view of
Moulay Idriss from
above on hillside
and across.

wahid    — 1
ithnein  — 2
thalatha - 3      lyoom -
aarba    — 4      today
khamsa   — 5
sitta    — 6      tomorrow-
seb'a    — 7      ghedda
timania  — 8
tes'a    — 9      yesterday
'ashra   — 10     ?
hadash   - 11
ithnash  - 12
thalatash - 13
'aarbatash - 14

and he made stabbing motions with the chamois cloth that he used to clean the car. We drove up a rough dirt road to a viewpoint overlooking the town. When asked if he would wait for us if we walked through the town, he declared he would but asserted that it would be a long wait as we would never return, so reluctantly we made do with the brief glimpse from afar. This is the only time I've encountered this sort of fear, aside from Italy where we met with much the same reaction when heading south to Sicily.

In Meknes now—an active town with a confusing medina. We've never been so bothered by hustlers but, taking the lesson learned from Fes, headed for the secondary gates away from the main entryway. We're getting into fights about which way to go; the pressure of being lost works against one strongly here.

And now we're here, I miss the thought of Layesh's presence even though I didn't see him again in Fes.

April 24/Rabat
Against better judgment we stayed two nights in Meknes. At one time Meknes was a great imperial city founded by another Moulay—Moulay Ismail. When Mohammed first drove us into Meknes, he described Moulay Ismail so vividly and so angrily that I had the wild impression that he was still alive, but no, he died in 1727. According to what I understood from Mohammed, heads used to regularly line the tops of the walls leading into the medina, and while I was there I found an old French newspaper with an illustration of this spectacle. But Moulay Ismail made a remarkable looking city: massive gates, huge gardens, impressive palaces. His mausoleum is so surrounded by guides that it is virtually impossible to get near it without hiring one.

Meknes now has the feel of a garrison town; it's rough in the new town, and the old town, which is quite a distance away, seems cut off and neglected. No, that makes it sound like it's deserted and it's anything but. Perhaps the best way of putting it is that attention has been focused on the palaces and gardens, making the rest of the city, both old and new, appear locked in a time warp.

Now off to arrange for Tunisian visas.

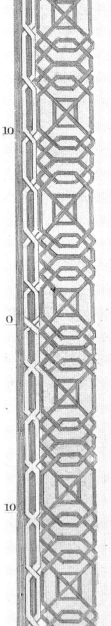

* Roll # 23
meknes
· Camera
cinema
ville
nouvelle
· residencies
old city
. market

10

, Expensive
hotel
3 ✳✳✳
Hotel meknes
224 DH !

0

15 DH
taxi ride
to 2nd try
entrance to
medina

l bareh -
yesterday

10

Hotel Figaro:
2** - very neat, very
faded (I think it has been
demoted to 1* - one of
the stars on the doors has
been partly scratched off)
crumbs on the mattress

- 104 DH

send pics

met in the Café Splendide:
Waiter and his fiancée
Najim el Hussein
and Sabira
22, rue dar Reghai
Salé

* Roll #24 (100 ASA)
· Casbah - casbah gdns.
· café, homes in casbah
· Bou Regreg river ;
across to the city of Salé

Later:
Rabat is very simple to negotiate, as all sections, including the old city, seem to be on a grid of sorts. We have no cause for disagreements now and nobody pays us the slightest attention. We found our way to the Tunisian consulate easily. Visas aren't necessary, but we didn't go away empty-handed—they loaded us up with tourist pamphlets.

Have spent most of the day in the medina and in the Casbah. The Casbah is a run-for-your-life dash across a busy ring road that surrounds the old city and overlooks the delta of the Bou Regreg River and Salé, Rabat's sister city on the other side of the river. Within the Casbah walls is a palace with incredible grounds. The gardens are a pleasant meeting place for groups of women, as well as a secure and secluded spot for discreet liaisons among young couples. The well-maintained gardens have a discipline that isn't immediately apparent, but after walking through and studying the layout of the walkways and the plantings I began to appreciate how complimentary the design of the garden is with the architecture. Formal, traditional filagree iron-work gates and window grates sit next to rough mud-washed walls. Cracked concrete steps lead to meticulously hand-painted doors. Carefully tended flower beds, rich with black loam, reveal hundreds of terra cotta shards, a testament to decades of broken pots. Also discovered a beautiful café near the palace gardens in the Casbah. The setting is much more spectacular than the menu (soft drinks, tea, and coffee), but we will probably go back there again tonight.

**RABAT**

Mètres
0   200   400   600

Trains from Rabat ville to Casablanca Port

7:00 (except Sat.)
7:30
7:53
8:20
9:23
10:45
11:33
12:05
12:35 (except Sun)
13:35
14:33
15:30
17:15
18:45

about a 55 minute trip.

Train station
kayn la gaar
كاين لجار

train
elmasheena
الماشينة

While we were dozing about the café this afternoon, I remembered to ask C what he meant by saying that he traveled because of his love of motion. He said "I remember what you're referring to, but I didn't say *motion*, I said *movement*." "What's the difference?" I asked. He didn't reply so I repeated my question. He said, rather impatiently, "It doesn't matter what the difference is, and anyway it doesn't matter what I said. I didn't mean it." What's *that* supposed to mean? I let the whole thing drop.

April 26, still Rabat
This is very weird and I think I'm starting to fall apart. We went to the Casbah café last night. There was a brief power outage and the whole café and street outside and the houses all around went dark. A loud "hurrah" from the patrons, nervous snickers and scraped chairs, and suddenly I feel quick pin pricks on my hand. Lights go back on and—I'm beside myself, I can barely write this—the design on my left hand is now extended up my wrist. The pin pricks feel like flea bites again but this time the coloring is blue, not red. It really looks like a tattoo; it is a tattoo. I want to take my nails to it and scratch it off, this infernal mess on my hand. Well, of course I'm looking around to see who might have done this to me but everyone is minding their own business, still laughing from the moment of darkness. I turn around and look hard at the man sitting immediately on my left. Could he have done it? His companion, facing me, is nudging the man, who now turns around. He says, "*Bon soir, madame,*" with a polite and

slightly interested look in his eye. An eye that roves up and down with speculation and assessment until it rests on Chris, and then the flicker definitely dies out. "Can I help you with something?" he continues in French. "No," I reply. "I didn't mean to disturb you, please excuse me."

Chris, who is day dreaming as usual, asks what all that was about. Fortunately, with him it isn't necessary to make up complicated explanations or excuses, the shrug of a shoulder is usually sufficient to dismiss almost any incident.

I can't believe that C hasn't said anything about the first design. Is it not visible? Is it visible only to me? Am I crazy? I've turned this into a game, to see how long it will take for questions to come up. A simple comment like, "Is your hand still bothering you?" would go a long way. Who cares anyway? If I told Chris that I was worried about it, he'd just come up with some practical explanation and make me feel like a fool. This is my problem, my secret, and has nothing to do with anyone else but me. Layesh knows what this tattoo means. He told me, I know he did. If only I could remember. I don't know what's happening to me. All I can do is wait to see what happens next. I'll photograph my hand again.

April 28
Have moved on to Casablanca. I've moved my watch to my right arm so every time I look at it I won't be reminded of the tattoo. We are staying in a faded old hotel, The Excelsior, once

Casablanca Hotels
·Staying at the Excelsior but also checked out:

·Hôtel Splendide
10, rue Chouia
unclassified but decent looking

· Grand Hotel
2 **
89 rue Oued El
    Makhazine
looks really great
and quieter

· Hôtel Royal
1 *
13, rue Mohammed
    El Qorri
-pretty average

· Georges V
Avenue des F.A.R.
2 **
150 DH
Nice desk clerk.

Found at the
Galerie d'Agdal
in Casablanca
-rue Poincaré
near the
Negresco Night
Club
---
45 DH

* Roll #26 (400 ASA)
In Casablanca
Art Deco bldgs
· Negresco
· Rue Nolly - apt
· various apts
· Sabir - sweeper

send
pic

~~Sabir el Mokhtar~~
Sabir el Mokhtar
c/o Hotel Excelsior
rue el Amraoui
Brahim, 2
Casablanca

Casablanca's place to be seen. It's quite noisy but I love its immense winding staircase, still-bustling lobby, and large, airy rooms. I'm wandering off on my own today as we have our eyes on different sections of the city, and C wants to pick up plane tickets to Tunis. I think we should go overland but he's insistent that we not waste the time. So I'm not going to make the arrangements. I don't want to leave Morocco anyway.

April 28—Back at the hotel
Why do I go off on my own? I just get into trouble. My hand is bandaged up and I have a bruise on my right temple and a headache that would wake the dead if it could scream. But I have to write this down before I forget. I wandered into the *suq* section to the north of the city center, a rather pathetic excuse for a market, which is apparent even if one is unaware of its origins as a French creation. However, outside of the market proper I found far more interesting makeshift markets, clearly set up for daily necessities and not for tourists. They are remarkable, seemingly made up of people, produce, and products

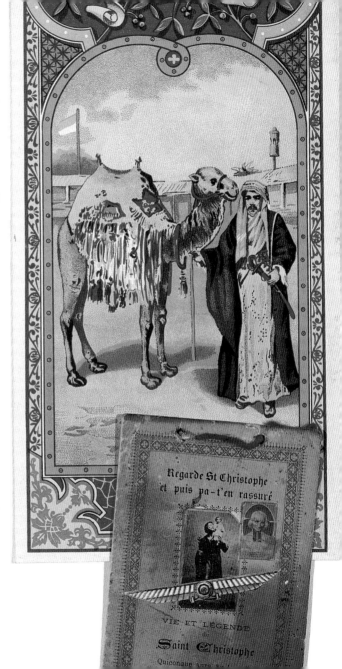

Regarde St Christophe
et puis va-t'en rassuré

VIE ET LÉGENDE
de
Saint Christophe

from everywhere in Morocco, not just from one city or region. The spice and medicine section made my mouth drop: not only were there the animal skins that we had seen in Fes but there were also whole, dead, stuffed lizards, gazelle heads, antlers, and stacks of cages full of live tortoises. And not just one or two shops, but shop after shop—small shanty huts, identical at first glance but really quite individual with their repugnant yet captivating wares. A large, noisy crowd had formed around a speaker at the outskirts and I naturally gravitated there to see what was going on. I stood for some minutes at the edge of the crowd and then lost interest. Political, or something. But as I turned away I was caught off balance by a surge in the crowd and was pushed against an iron grating set into the wall of a store. My first instinct wasn't of fear, but to try to keep the camera from hitting the wall or jamming into the bars. Then as I held onto the grate another push from the crowd swept me along ripping the skin off the back of my left hand. It was terrible and frightening to be so helpless. I fell down and hit my head on something. A couple of Moroccan women and a young man rushed over to me and picked me up. They took me to a nearby pharmacy where I was given endless cups of tea and an arm-length of bandages.

A typical case of being at the wrong place at the wrong time. It wasn't anything against me, I was simply in the way and suffered

*  Roll #26 27 (400 ASA)
· Hotel staircase
· Hotel room (#34)
· Market

ana - I
enta (m) - you
enti (f) - you
huwa - he/it
heeya - she/it
we - hena
ntooma - you (pl.)
huma - they

the consequences. The pharmacist told me that the speaker was a hadj—that word again—and that he was preaching, so it was better to have made myself scarce anyway.

So now I have this bandage from knuckles to elbow on my tattoo hand, which hurts like hell. Maybe the abrasion will get rid of the pattern once and for all. I just wish I could know what it means.

Now to get rid of the headache.

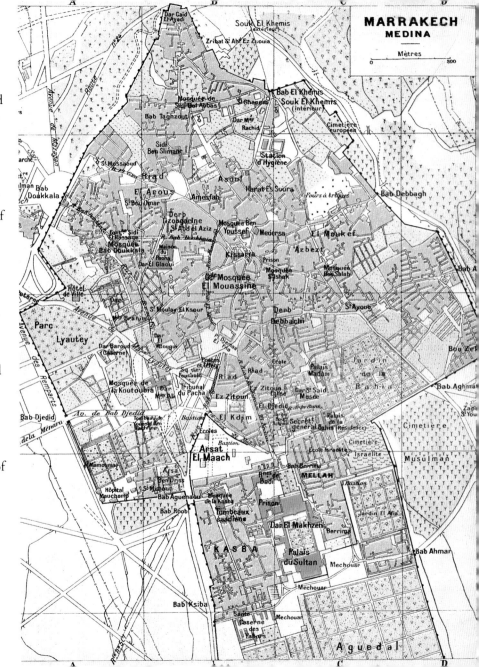

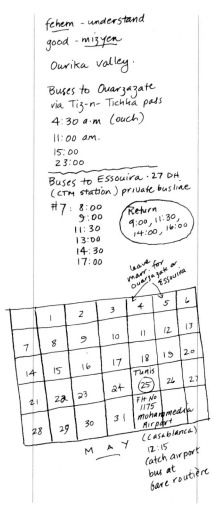

fehem - understand
good - mizyen

Ourika valley.

Buses to Ouarzazate
via Tiz-n- Tichka pass
4:30 a.m (ouch)
11:00 am.
15:00
23:00

Buses to Essouira · 27 DH
(CTM station) private bus line
#7: 8:00        Return
    9:00       9:00, 11:30,
    11:30      14:00, 16:00
    13:00
    14:30
    17:00

leave for
marrazate or
Essouira

| | 1 | 2 | 3 | 4 | 5 | 6 |
| 7 | 8 | 9 | 10 | 11 | 12 | 13 |
| 14 | 15 | 16 | 17 | 18 | 19 | 20 |
| 21 | 22 | 23 | 24 | Tunis (25) | 26 | 27 |
| 28 | 29 | 30 | 31 | FH No 1175 mohammedia Airport (casablanca) | | |

M A Y

12:15
catch airport
bus at
gare routière

April 29, Marrakech

Moved on as soon as possible. Casablanca is too noisy and dirty, not worth more than a day. Fortunately lots of trains depart for Marrakech from the station nearby. C has asked what happened yesterday in Casablanca. I said I injured my hand in the market but nothing else. It seems imperative to keep this to myself.

We wandered through the Marrakech markets. All I remember are swirls of brightly colored wool draped over rods spanning the roofs on either side of the alleyways. And I can still hear the echoes of loud voices close to me. My hand is no longer painful but a numbness is spreading and it's infecting my mind. It's turned a country full of light and air into a corner of stifling darkness.

May 1

I've undone the bandages—this is stranger than I could ever believe. The tattoo has grown and it now snakes part way up my arm almost to my elbow. It looks like part of a map. I can see cities and towns, river valleys and mountain ranges. And I can see eyes and hands—talismans to ward away evil? What evil? Perhaps that which I might find if I follow the route on the map. This is what Layesh showed me in the café; this is what he was trying to tell me. This is a gift that I must accept, not a threat to be avoided.

I'll keep the bandages on—how could I explain this to C?

I walk carefully as if stepping on eggs, prepared at all costs to protect this hazy film spreading across my body.

May 2

The map is now growing visibly, I can see it, and it has crept above the elbow. I am spending the afternoon sitting by myself in the hotel room just staring at it. I thought that getting away from the glare on the streets, from the pretense of conversation with Chris, from the pressure of the hustlers, would give me some time to think. But I am just sitting and watching the tangle of lines on my skin. It's beautiful, but it's ugly, too, like the veins and arteries that you can trace on the inside of your wrist. My arm no longer belongs to me. It's become another thing—to be admired and studied but not a functional object. It no longer carries my watch; it feels too precious to be made to hold things and I can't bear to touch myself in case it spreads even further. As I become detatched from it, I can admire and appreciate its physical beauty as though it *were* a map drawn out over months of exploration and study, but the moment I remember it's mine, a part of me, I reel with nausea.

The way I'm sitting, I can see the map unfold, as if I were on a journey sped up five times, maybe ten times, I don't know—fast. Everything is racing by. I move rapidly from desert to town, past stony plains destitute of growth to rich verdant oases. The sun is beating down hot wherever I am, whether it's day or night. Swarms of flies just brushed past my face, their wings beating against my skin. They're gone. I hurtle past crowds of people and catch splinters of languages I've never heard before, the smell of roasting meat, the air thick with spices, blood, and dust. I sweep into train stations and bus stations, and now and then a town I know or knew is called out—a destination—but I move on, into libraries where the millions of words I read echo in my ears from right to left, where pages and books crumble around me scattering dust and paper into the air like millions of moths. I rush through the cold, vast cathedrals of Europe and feel my bones turning dry and brittle like those who are buried in their depths. I race along the ocean's edge feeling the ice and the damp of the north and the heat and the damp of the equator. The salt sticks to my nostrils and cakes my hair; the creatures from the sea ride with me for awhile, then drop off back into the water as I turn inland. I fly through the fondouks of Africa filling my pockets with grains and fruits from endless caravans, and as I pass the traders join me just long enough to trace their routes onto my map.

I am using a camera that I don't understand, and I am taking photographs that I have already seen.

I am drawing the map on my body with a tiny pen and with a penmanship so light and delicate that it makes me weep. Fragile leaves sprout through the cracked earth where my tears have fallen, so again I move on quickly lest my tears take root where I stand.

But the tears turn to steam, and I am suddenly no longer moving but in a dark, cavernous room surrounded by figures—women—shrouded by the fog and steam of my weeping. As I lay on a rough stone block I can feel myself being pummeled and massaged and a voice, in a foreign language, says over and over,

"We'll rub this off, then you won't have to leave again. We'll rub this off." I watch the map peel off in one piece and slither to the floor. The women emerge from the dark corners and slowly walk, bent over double and with arms outstretched, towards my map lying on the damp tiles. I sit up and watch them coming closer and closer, and then, suddenly afraid and cold, I grab the map, step into it one foot after the other. I draw it on like the skin of a cheetah, pull it up over my shoulders, stick my arms into it, until I am once again totally enveloped. The women begin to wail, and I understand, I finally understand, I have something they want. I had been someone chosen, but now I am someone who has made a choice. Secure in my map I leave, as rapidly as I came, and my last sight of the room is the image of the women returning to their darknesses and silences, confined by the steam left by my tears.

The map does indeed cover my whole body now. I've brushed out a couple of flies tangled up in my hair and licked the taste of salt from my lips. When is this going to stop?

May 4
Was at the French library all yesterday afternoon going through atlases. I can't find any reference to the area the tattoo shows, so it must be old. Have to do some more research. Am now sitting at one of the cafés by the square reading through some books I borrowed from

5TH   CALL ✓
      CONSULATE
CALL POLICE? ✓

6TH

POLICE STN.
JEMMA ELEFNA
NEAR CLUB
MEDITERRANEE

BRING PHOTO,
I.D.

S'IL VOUS PLAIT -
JE VOUDRAY PARLER
A HMID ABD ALLAH
JE M'APPELLE...
MON NUMERO DE
TELEPHONE EST
QUATRE-
DEUX-
HUIT-
NEUF-
UN-
CINQ

43-67-79
MARRAKECH POLICE

JE NE
COMPRENDS
PAS

HMID ABD ALLAH

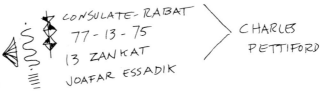

CONSULATE - RABAT
77 - 13 - 75
13 ZANKAT
JOAFAR ESSADIK

CHARLES
PETTIFORD

JOAPHAR
JOAFAR →

ALLEN: FES 63 - 38 - 93

Message:
CALL M. MAURICE ROBILLARD
CASABLANCA PARIS NEWSPAPER
38 - 50 - 00
FORGET IT!

May 7, Marrakech:
Lydia's disappeared. She's been missing since the 4th of May.

May 8, Marrakech:
She's still gone.

She left her luggage, her books, and her camera. This journal was found at a café along with a couple of library books. The café owner saw me pass by yesterday and gave it to me. He wanted to give me the library books as well, but I brushed him off, I'm sorry to say. All she has is her passport, money, and the plane ticket to Tunis that I bought in Casablanca. It's incredible. Marrakech is a small place. Most of the shopkeepers around our hotel recognized us after the second day—no one could go missing here.

I've reported this to the police and telephoned the consulate in Rabat. Also asked the guy at the consulate to phone the police and talk to them, as I think I didn't make myself very clear. They've both advised me to stay put for an indefinite period of time. She could be hurt or abducted, I suppose, but Lydia just doesn't get herself into dangerous situations. Or, at least, if she gets into them, she gets herself out of them. The consulate told me that the police will check hospitals as a matter of course.

May 9, Marrakech:
It occurred to me last night to read through this journal in case there are some clues as to why Lydia vanished. I haven't been

✓

MAY 8
· NEED TO FIND PASSPORT
  (WHERE IN HELL'S NAME
   WILL I FIND THAT?)

· EXTRA PHOTOS

· INTERPRETER?
  CHECK W/ TOURIST OFFICE
  SEE IF GUIDE WILL DO.

· FLIGHT INFO. ✓

· FLIGHT TO TUNIS —
  # 1175
  MOHAMMEDIA
  AIRPORT @ 12:15
  ROYAL AIR MAROC

following her writing, no reason to. I'm shocked. I never noticed a tattoo on her hand, ever. It's all fiction. And when she came back after being away all day in Casablanca she had the bandages on her hand, but she said it was from scraping them on rough stone. It certainly didn't sound serious.

I was kind of hurt by some of the things she wrote. I'm not arrogant. How devastating it is to be thought of as arrogant. Surely, we've known each other long enough, and well enough, for her to understand that my silence only reflects my sense of trust and satisfaction?

The police have asked if she left any addresses or contacts or suggestions of where she might have gone but I can't show them this journal. They'll think she's lost her mind.

Why would she make this up?

May 10, still Marrakech:
Looks like I'll be here for a few days more at least. I'm going crazy. They want me to stay another week in case she shows up on her own. I think it is more formality than anything else. They've notified the sea and airports and the Moroccan airlines in case she cashes in her ticket. The police wanted to know if we fought or at least disagreed about anything. All I know is that she wasn't herself since Casablanca, but it was nothing that would account for her leaving.

I've given them the names of the hotels we stayed at and of acquaintances, including Allen and Abderrahman.

ANOTHER MESSAGE
FROM ROBILLARD
AT CASA
PARIS

I'm going up the wall here. Making the rounds over and over to any place she might have been. Sitting in the café she last wrote about, every afternoon. I can't stand the way the waiter moons over me and pats my shoulder.

May 11:
The police have left a message with the desk clerk for me to go see them—maybe there's some news.

later:
No real news. Just a report that two books had been found in the café overlooking the Djemaa el Fna square and had been returned to the French library. They asked me to go over to the library and see if they were the books Lydia had borrowed. I went—it passes time. I couldn't tell; I didn't get a good look at them before. They were heavy volumes of geographical data on the Maghreb area. Interesting stuff. Great old charts of sea levels and shale deposits. But, if they were books that she took out, I don't know what she'd have expected to find. I suppose that the waiter (or whoever) at the café didn't tell the police that he had tried to give me the books before.

I was curious how Lydia was able to borrow books from this library. It didn't strike me as the kind of place that would lend out books readily. So I asked the librarian. He shook his head and said, quite disapprovingly, that she hadn't checked them out. Just walked out with them. And then to leave them at a café and such

*The past is inscribed and the future defined,*
*As thoroughly on my flesh as in my mind.*

valuable books! I think she's made his day—frankly, it looks pretty boring in there. They need a scandal or two to keep things lively. There was a note stuck in one of them, which I pinched.

The police think that I have been particularly unhelpful. They've also started to appear quite confused about our relationship.

May 15, Casablanca:
Police suggested I return here in case she comes back for the flight out to Tunis, so I'm at the Excelsior again. I think the suggestion was made in order to get me off their backs so they can get back to real important work like collecting bribes. It's awful here—the clerks keep asking me where Madame is. I tried saying that she was meeting me later, but the police have been here so they know. Now I get phone calls from the hotel staff asking solicitously if I want anything from room service, or if I've had any news of Madame, or telling me anxiously that there is an urgent message from this person or that, perhaps there's news . . .

Everyone here knows the day she may show up, the day we are supposed to leave—even the waiter knows. Yesterday the sweeper reminded me that she promised to send a copy of the photo she took of him. As I flip again through this journal I see more and more obligations to write and send photos, get in touch with far-off relatives of people I can't even remember meeting. When did she talk to all of these people?

I would rather change hotels but this is a place where she may try to contact me. I've considered the possibility that she left unwillingly or has been in an accident, but I can't accept it. In her writing she seemed sure of being on the edge of something—I am more positive than ever that she has left of her own accord. The police have also suggested that she may have mixed herself up in something that backfired, but think it unlikely as well. Tourists, I have been told, are remarkably safe in Morocco, and I believe it.

Later:
Dropped into the consulate's office. They've been in daily contact with the airlines—the ticket hasn't been cashed in yet. We were due to leave May 25th, so they'll continue checking till then.

The police told me that the address she had for the Café Metropol in Fes, on the Boulevard du Quatrième Tirailleurs, doesn't exist anymore, that the street name changed in 1956. I remember now that she noticed that too. She wrote that the man she claimed was the café owner, Layesh, wrote it down for her. I remember that strange conversation we had with Abderrahman when she insisted that she had spoken to the owner. I thought she would never let up.

THE DESK CLERK GAVE THIS TO
ME THIS A.M. SO THIS IS
WHAT M. ROBILLARD WANTED.
COULDN'T EVEN GET THE
DATE RIGHT.

## UNE ÉTRANGÈRE A DISPARU

MARRAKECH

La police de Marrakech a signalé la disparition d'une étrangère s'appellant Lydia Usher. Elle voyageait avec son ami, Christopher Ward, quand elle a disparu le 5 mai.

Voici son signalement : âgée de trente ans, taille 1,60 m, yeux marrons, cheveux courts et bruns. La dernière fois qu'on l'a vue, elle portait un gilet bleu brodé, des sandales et des blue-jeans. Ses effets personnels sont restés à l'hôtel.

La police a retracé sa route le 5 mai et a découvert qu'elle avait visité la Bibliothèque Française, av Mohammed V, pendant la matinée, et qu'ensuite elle

(suite page 2, col 3)

était restée longtemps au Café Agdal à Djemaa el Fna. Le garçon de café a déclaré qu'elle avait passé son temps à lire.

Jusqu'ici aucune malveillance n'est soupçonnée. M Ward restera au Maroc encore quelques semaines en attendant des nouvelles de son amie.

Si vous avez quelques renseignements au sujet de cette femme, appelez la police de Marrakech à 67-79 ou venez au bureau à Djemaa el Fna. L'anonymat sera respecté.

M.R.

May 17, Casablanca still:
I telephoned Allen yesterday to tell him of Lydia's disappearance.
He'd already heard from the police and suggested I come up to Fes
for a few days. I'll think about it.

It's just occurred to me that after all her haranguing, Lydia has
finally got me to write a journal. Nothing else new today.

May 18, Casablanca:
The plane ticket still isn't cashed so I still have to wait. I might as
well go to Fes. I feel like there isn't anything left here to hold
me—that once she disappeared it was a message for me to leave.
I'm putting in time, spending money. Took her camera around
and shot off a few photos. There's an amazing amount of exposed
film in her bag waiting to be developed. She kept harping on how
nobody knows how to process film properly so I'll wait till I get
back home—this'll cost a fortune though. Went to the harbor and
then wandered around the medina for the afternoon. I must admit
I would rather be stuck in Marrakech.
    I'm getting pretty irritated. This better not be her idea of a
joke—it just isn't funny. I've put up with her stupid sense of
humor in the past, but nothing as rotten as this. Things she's done
before—all kid stuff—like the time she sent me the fake telegram
ordering me to report for military service. Shit. I've got no obliga-
tion to hang around. I could leave tomorrow. She's done this
deliberately. Made up the stuff about a map to unnerve me.

تـــصريح بضيـــــــاع
ــــــــــــــــــــــ

اشهــــد انــــا السيـد اكريسطــوفير ورد بـالاشــارة الـى فقـدات او ضيــاع
السيــــدة ليـد بيـا أوشيــــر بالبـالغــــة مـن العمــر 30 سنـــة مـن جنسيـة اجنبيــــة
وذلك مـا بيــن 3-4 و 5 مـايـو بمـدينــــة مراكــــش.
ان هـذا الاقـــرار هو تـصريح معلـلا بافعــال تتـعلـق بفقـدان السيـدة المذكـورة
صحيحـة ولا مجـال الشـك فيهـا . ولقـد صـرح بـذلك الـى السلطـة المغـربيـة .

امضــــــاء .............. التاريــــخ .............

بمـدينــة ............

FLIMSY OF MY DECLARATION
OF LYDIA'S DISAPPEARANCE
"FOR MY RECORDS"

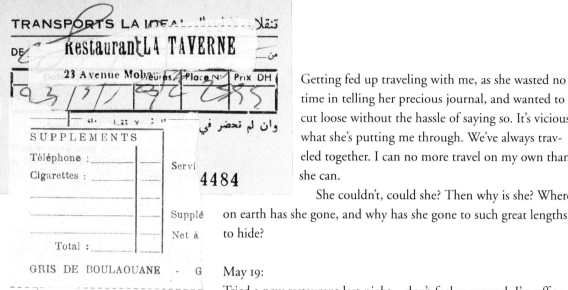

Getting fed up traveling with me, as she wasted no time in telling her precious journal, and wanted to cut loose without the hassle of saying so. It's vicious what she's putting me through. We've always traveled together. I can no more travel on my own than she can.

She couldn't, could she? Then why is she? Where on earth has she gone, and why has she gone to such great lengths to hide?

May 19:

Tried a new restaurant last night—don't feel very good. I'm off to Fes this afternoon.

May 20, Fes:

Have taken it easy for the last few days and tried to forget my bad feelings about Lydia. Allen and I went to the Metropol and saw Abderrahman, who asked after Lydia. He seems genuinely distraught, as if her disappearance was his fault, since the police questioned him and claimed that he wrote the wrong address in her journal. He told me that he hadn't written a thing in Lydia's book regardless of what she stated. I showed him the address (I now carry the journal around with me like some kind of talisman), and he appeared to be quite surprised. The name in the journal—Layesh—isn't his name, he says. It's his father's, and he confirmed what Lydia had discovered—that the address was the café's old address. We've now been invited to his home so that he can show the page to his mother. As his father is long dead, I can't help but think that this is going to upset her, seeing her dead husband's name written in a foreigner's diary. But we're—Allen and I—going to his house in Fes el Djedid this evening. This is really confusing.

Later:

Well, stranger and stranger. We went to Abderrahman's apartment and met his family—his wife, a couple of children, and his mother. I can't stretch this out, I'm not like Lydia—I gave Abderrahman the journal, which he passed to his mother. She had brought out some letters or bills or something—her dead husband's writing at any rate—and compared the two. What followed—Christ. Shrieks and wailing. Thank God Allen was with me. It was everything I could do to wrestle the diary out of her hands; she was going to rip it up. I got up to grab it when I realized what she intended to do, Abderrahman jumped up to calm her down, and Allen danced about making sure I didn't commit some irreparable gaffe. To top it off the children started crying, and Abderrahman's wife yelled at them to be quiet. Finally, I got the journal tucked away safely into my jacket's inner pocket. Abderrahman hustled us over to the front door and asked us to wait in the hallway for a minute. I was all for leaving straight away, but Allen reminded me that he'll be living here for another

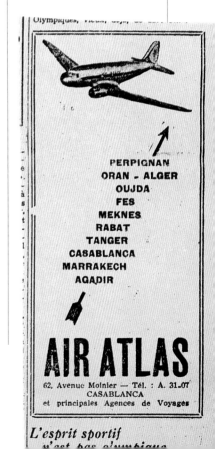

20TH
156 — HOTEL
120 — CAFE
15 — TAXI
80 — DINNER
20 — SNACK
___
283   $35 — ?!
    8)283
     24
     ___
     43

year, so we waited uneasily. The shrieks from inside the apartment finally quieted down but not before some of the neighbors came out to ask what the matter was. Allen's Arabic isn't too bad to my ears, although he says it's rudimentary, and he seemed to have a diplomatic answer at hand. Whatever he said provoked interest, however, and before long there were five or six people crammed into the dim, narrow hallway with us.

Abderrahman came out into the hall, exchanged greetings with his neighbors, and then motioned for us to leave the building with him. We got into his car, and he drove us to his café, talking non-stop in an impossible-to-follow mix of Arabic and French. Combined with Allen's translations into English and ceaseless horn honking, there wasn't a moment of silence.

Anyway, he repeated what he had been saying, several times, once we got to the café, and he brought the letters that his mother had been looking at. I don't know. It could be the same handwriting, but the fact is it simply isn't possible and that's that.

Allen thinks he's got this all figured out but he wants to read through Lydia's journal. Oh sure, I'm going to hand it to him with that stuff she wrote about him being a bit of a nerd. I told him it's too personal, that she'd rip me to shreds if I ever let someone else read it. He's been after me all day about this and I doubt that he'll let up. It was a mistake, that "personal" remark; it has him *really* interested.

He's always nagging me to marry Lydia, or at least live with her again, or just break the whole thing off—thinks our friendship isn't healthy. He thinks that it keeps me from committing myself, from becoming responsible. It hasn't occurred to him that perhaps this isn't my choice, that maybe Lydia has had a lot to do with this. She has always controlled the way that we live, the way that we travel, both when we were together and now that we aren't any longer. Anyway, all that is ancient history and I can't return to the past and change things.

At any rate, he really wants me to be some kind of sleuth hero. But I'm packing up after the 25th. Mystery or not, one thing I do know now, she won't be on the flight. She's gone.

Abderrahman offered to give me one of the letters; in fact, he insisted. But I refused to take it, assuring him that I was convinced that the handwriting was identical. What would I do with such a letter—take it to the police as proof that a dead man lured Lydia away? Abderrahman says he was seven years old when the letter was written in 1941 so that makes him about 57 now. Which makes his mother about 75—I'm ashamed to have grabbed the diary away from her. He also said that he was nine years old when his father disappeared. Everyone assumes he's dead, but no one ever heard for sure. They advertised for him in the papers in Morocco and in France, and they had a memorial service in 1950 when they finally gave up. Abderrahman offered to take me to the cemetery to show me the tomb. I've declined. Nonetheless—it couldn't have been his father who signed his name in Lydia's book even if he were still alive. He'd be a fossil now, not the distinguished middle-aged man we both saw in Tangier. I'm so confused—just let me go home.

21ST

TELEGRAM      —   15DH
  TO RABAT
PLANT              10
CAFE               20
TAXI               10
TIPS               10
HOTEL             156
LUNCH              40
                  ———
    $32           261
  8|261
    24
    21
    16
    50

2 CARPETS - $225
  LAMP      $56
  P/O       $40
WRAPPING    $5
           ————
           $326

CARPETS @ $ 112
            × 6
          $672
      SELL @ $750

---

May 21:

Went to the Metropol this morning to apologize to Abderrahman. Asked Allen last night what kind of gift I should buy to atone for my behavior; on his advice I brought a house plant with me.

Abderrahman brushed aside the apology, accepted the plant, and invited me back over for dinner, saying that his mother, too, is embarrassed and would also like to apologize. He told me to bring Allen, so I'll call him to see if he can make it. I sat down for a cup of coffee and spent an amusing fifteen minutes watching Abderrahman walk around his café—hustling the lone waiter, talking with friends, going to the door and yelling at some kids hanging out on the street—all with that dumb plant under his arm. It turns out that Abderrahman knows a couple of antique dealers I didn't run into before, so I'm spending the rest of the day finishing up the last few items on my buying list. Then there will truly be nothing keeping me here.

May 21, later:

The consulate has asked that I postpone my departure until the 28th so they can fill out all the necessary forms should Lydia not reappear.

Allen is free tonight so I'm meeting him at the Metropol at 7 pm and we'll go with Abderrahman over to his apartment.

May 22, Casablanca:

Last night went smoothly. We were all on our best behavior.

Abderrahman's mother apologized, I apologized, we all shook hands, even Allen. We had dinner, and then she asked again about the journal. I took it out of my pocket and handed it to Abderrahman to give to her. He asked me to open it to the correct page, which I did, and then he showed her the page again without actually giving her the book. She had been perched, looking quite uncomfortable, on the low couch that ran around the perimeter of the small living room. We were all sitting pretty much knee to knee, quite relaxed and unconcerned about bumping into one another. But she shielded her legs from being touched even by the children. The couch was quite saggy, and in spite of her ramrod posture, her knees still seemed to come up to her chin. In her lap she held onto a small, carved wooden box that was jammed with paper. When Abderrahman showed her the journal she reread the name and address, nodded, pulled out one of the sheets of paper, a letter, and instead of getting upset, she smiled. A really contented smile like she'd been given a wonderful gift. She got up with great difficulty, as she was still holding onto the box, leaned towards me over the low table in the center of the room, and said something—Allen said she blessed me. Then she reached across, took my hand lightly in her own dry, thin one, pressed it almost imperceptibly, and released it, raising her hand to her lips and then down to her breast. Then she left the room.

She came back about five minutes later with a small photograph, which she gave to me. It was a photo reproduction, Abderrahman explained, of his father and another man, dressed in

Farjallah Haik    Layesh Boussalem

traditional clothing. His father, Layesh, was the man on the right. The photograph was taken in 1942, the year before he disappeared.

It is a likeness of the man we saw in Tangier—but handsome, middle-aged Mediterranean men seem to have a certain similarity. And the change to European clothing makes quite a difference. At any rate—it's ridiculous—the man we saw could not be Layesh, Abderrahman's father, in spite of the name. I tried to give the photo back. The mother gestured that I should keep it, so I have it now—a souvenir, I suppose, to paste into this journal. Too bad I didn't keep the letter, after all.

I get no sense from the family what they think of all this, of why there appears to be some connection between their dead father/husband and a foreigner. I asked Allen but he said he has no idea.

I'm not that interested in all this talking to people—I hope Lydia realizes what she's making me do.

May 25, Casablanca:
Just a few more hours before I have to be at the airport. Can't book a ticket back to London until I find out what happens this afternoon. Consul's assistant thinks I'm a cold fish—he told me as much yesterday. Said that most people in my situation would be quite upset—as if I'm not. I suppose blubbering in public is a

quick way to get sympathy and maybe a bit more action, but it's cheap. Cheap and vulgar.

later:
So that's that. No show, but I knew it. I've booked a flight to London and from there back home. No point hanging around.

May 26:
Phoned Allen to say goodbye and he tried again to talk me into staying. He doesn't understand that there is nothing here for me, that the only reason that I remained was the unrealistic hope that maybe she'd turn up. So I'll do the formalities at the consulate and the police station. After a great deal of effort and getting cut off I talked to the Marrakech police this morning to thank them for their efforts. If this weren't so sickening I could almost laugh at the phone system and my feeble attempts to shout in French, but really it just adds to the desperation I feel. I don't belong here—this country leaves me cold. I don't know, maybe even though I knew that it was futile to wait, maybe I really thought there was some hope. Maybe that's why I'm so crushed now. To be honest, I don't know what is worse, really, to think that I have been abandoned, or to think that Lydia is dead.

May 27:
Feel a bit better today. Started sorting through stuff

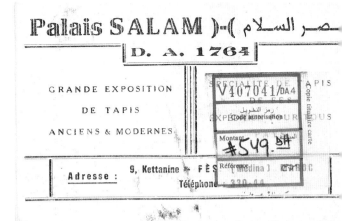

Palais SALAM )-( صر السلام

D. A. 1764

GRANDE EXPOSITION
DE TAPIS
ANCIENS & MODERNES

V407041/DA4

Montant #549.

Adresse : 9, Kettanine - FÈS (Medina)
Téléphone 330.44

25TH
AIRPORT BUS    20 DH
HOTEL          180
TAXI           10
TIPS           5
LUNCH          25
AIRPORT BUS    20
               ───
               260
DINNER         80
               ───
               340
               ═══

Table N° 6      Date

Glace - Brasserie - Café - Restaurant

"Petit Poucet"

Maison fondée en 1920

الدار البيضاء / مطار محمد الخامس
CASABLANCA / AEROPORT MOHAMMED V

26TH
L.D.    #1204
HOTEL   180
LUNCH   40
L.D     15
L.D     12
NEWSP.  7
DINNER  80
        ———
        344

PALAIS ES-SEBA
RUE DES FRERES
(WON'T MAIL)

ANTIQUED FRAMES
  × 3 = $78.00

BIRD CAGE = $24.00

TILES  $6.00 × 8 = $48.00

PAINTING
  (1924)    $124.00
  (OIL)
          ———
          $274

trying to see what could be left behind—after all I now have two sets of luggage, light though each may be for one person. I'll mail the extra stuff home along with the last of the purchases I've made. I've worked my way through almost the entire list except for a couple of items. It's pretty much paid for my whole trip.

Last minute message from the Marrakech police. They've misplaced her photo—could I send another one? It'll have to be from home. I'll have to try to remember to send them one.

May 28, 11 am:
On the plane to London. The airline is really crazy: they let the smokers on first. They're supposed to fill up the last rows, and then when they're seated they let the nonsmokers on, who rush up to the front of the plane. Of course, anyone like me who thinks that rushing and pushing is dismal behavior gets stuck one row up from the smoking section. I'd hate to commute on this airline.

This is the first time I've actually had a chance to really look at the photo that Abderrahman's mother gave me. It's clearly a studio shot of the "colorful local inhabitants," gracefully staged and tastefully vignetted. Layesh was an incredibly good-looking man. I was told that he often posed for the local photographer to help him out and that the images were usually sold as postcards. Abderrahman's mother had laughed at the costumes and had dismissed them as "Algerian" in quite an insulting tone.

Below both figures someone carefully wrote their names in roman script. I've tucked the photo back into the journal.

I never imagined that journal writing could be so addictive. Now it feels like anything I forget to write down didn't actually happen.

June 3:

Back home. Might as well continue this journal, as it seems the trip isn't over yet. Of course, I had a lot of explaining to do when I told everyone the news. They all blasted me and are right: I should have called and told them, especially her mother and father. But how could I tell her parents that I knew the last people Lydia would turn to for help would be her family. I don't recall one time, in all the years that we've known each other, that either of her parents voluntarily asked anything about where we'd been or what we'd seen. Once when we came back after being away for three months her mother was surprised to find out that we had been away at all. This really is Lydia's fault as much as her family's. I've been the one sending the postcards to her parents for some time now, not Lydia. I half suspect they aren't read. I don't think this bothers Lydia at all; she easily replaces affections as she moves from place to place, picking up new family and friends without any effort whatsoever. No, she would never have got in touch with her real home; she had too many substitutes closer at hand. It doesn't help that people here are hurt as well as frightened and anxious about her disappearance. And I feel like a heel for

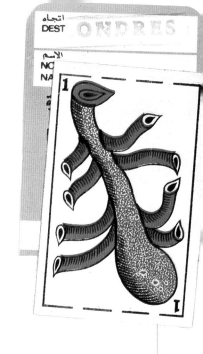

DEST ONDRES

Health Alert No
For International Travelers Arriving in t

To The Traveler
Keep this card in your wallet or purs
become ill during this time, give this card
and tell him/her about your recent trave
States.

coming back just three weeks later. I keep asking myself, could I have helped by staying there? I think I've redeemed myself somewhat by telling her parents that I would return to Morocco should there be any sign that I would be useful.

Her father was set to go himself, but I have talked him out of that for the time being.

I sat with her family last night going over the journal and the photo and letter and books. There isn't any point holding back information. They don't have a clue about her life ordinarily, so this is far beyond anything that they could ever comprehend. I showed them the ephemera she had collected so far on this trip—a large envelope of cast-off paper and broken bits of ceramics and junk, and everyone laughed and asked when she had started doing this. They shook their heads, amazed to find out that she's done this as long as I've known her—since school, when she lived at home—and they didn't have any idea. I asked her mother when she'd last been to Lydia's apartment, and she admitted that she had never been there. I'm toying with the idea of taking her over there tomorrow, then she'll really see what kind of pack rat her daughter is. On second thought maybe I won't. I can't take care of the whole family.

Rereading the journal—Lydia was, is, a heathen. She wrote that I washed her clothes because of the fleas. She didn't write: I washed her clothes *all* of the time. Once, one winter, when I met her in Paris after she had traveled on her own through Italy and France for a month, the stench was disagreeable to say the least. She'd washed maybe two or three times during her whole trip. Her excuse—too cold to take her clothes off. Disagreeable is a mild word.

I'll drop off the film tomorrow. There are over 20 rolls of black-and-white—all shot off in just over a month. Photography doesn't much interest me usually but I'm definitely impatient to see these photographs.

There was quite a lot of mail waiting for me at my apartment in spite of the fact that everyone had been told we would be away for six months. Usually when I get home after a long trip, the first thing I do is reacquaint myself with my collection. I'm so proud of it. This time I glanced around and saw a lot of tacky crap. I can't feel that way, I won't let myself, so I quickly sifted through the envelopes, holding my breath in case there was a letter from Lydia, and then left and went and stayed the first night in her apartment.

I'm back in my own apartment now and have overcome my initial reaction, but there's a lingering aftertaste that keeps me from the pleasure I usually experience at being home.

What to do next? Allen would have some ideas. Without Allen here I feel like I'm on my own in a major way. Family and friends will need some time to get over the shock before they'll be able to accept the unusual circumstances of her disappearance, so they're no help. I don't know what I can achieve from here, but the buying worked out so well on this trip that I'll be able to

ACTION PHOTOGRAPHICS
654 - 7211
$10 /ROLL TO DEVELOP
  AND MAKE CONTACT
    SHEETS
(SAME 120 & 35 MM)

MARSDEN & ASSOC.
627 - 9212
$10.50/ DEV. & CONT.
(SAME DAY SERVICE)

CONTACT PHOTO (BILL)
777 - 2154
$9.25 /ROLL

$9.25

NOON

afford to take more time off to really look into this. Look into what? For heaven's sake, a woman disappears in Morocco, her chum hightails it back to safety. What can I find out here that I couldn't find out in Morocco? Oh well, maybe it's some of Allen's enthusiasm rubbing off after all. A little late.

June 5:
I have the film back and it did cost a fortune. It's almost all black and white except for a few rolls of slides, so I have over 25 sheets of contact prints to sort through.

June 6:
A lot happened yesterday. Aside from picking up the contact sheets and developed negatives I mailed a couple of photos of Lydia to the consulate in Rabat and the police in Marrakech. Now that I have the contact sheets I see that I should have waited and sent one of the more recent photos that someone (not me) took of her with her camera.

I spent the better part of the afternoon putting the contact sheets into chronological order and marking those photos that are to be sent to various people. I don't think I'll be able to correctly match all the names with all of the faces but maybe it would be amusing for them to receive photos of complete strangers—a sort of chain photo letter—"pass this photo to the next name on the list and after three months you will receive a copy of your own photo."

This housekeeping process is helping me to avoid thinking about these photographs which represent what was to have been a reasonably happy and interesting six-month trip. To look at the places that she has photographed but that we saw together is making me uncharacteristically sentimental. She has photographed all of the hotel rooms we stayed in, hotel and restaurant staff from London to Marrakech, gardens we whiled away hours in, and especially the sites and vistas that remain mysteriously unrecorded in her journal. It is odd, looking back, how few references there are to daily sight-seeing, almost as if the days were spent in active attempts to stay away from anything remotely related to tourism.

But the photographs reassure me that, although not written into the journal, we did in fact make good use of our time.

June 7:

I finished matching the names of the people she promised to send photos to with the photographs. An orderly list of the names and addresses (30 in all, imagine the list at the end of six months!) with a second column for the contact sheet number and a third for the exposure number.

There are many photos that I can't place, taken while she wandered off on her own, and there are photographs of what must be her hand sprinkled throughout the contact sheets. I can't see anything marked on the hands in the photographs.

ROLL #1
TAXI DRIVER —
ARNIE SIMPSON
— NO ADDRESS.

ROLL #? — NOT NUMBERED
TRIP FROM LDN.
BUS DRIVER —
MARIAN ÷ LEWIS
PETTIGREW ✓
BUS DRIVER —
MARCEL CONTI ✓
. LOOK FOR RECEIPT.

AHMED ABD ES SALAM
— ROLL #2 ✓
HOTEL KASBA

ANGLICAN CHURCH } ROLL
KEEPER } #4
— NAME ?

ROLL #6 —
SOUAL BEN AARBA
✓

ROLL #8 — MOH. ✓
BOUTAIB

MOHAN ÷ RABAI
LAST NAME ?! ⇒ ?
ADDRESS —
✓ BAB EL FTOUH ?

GOOD GRIEF. I'VE
ONLY JUST STARTED.

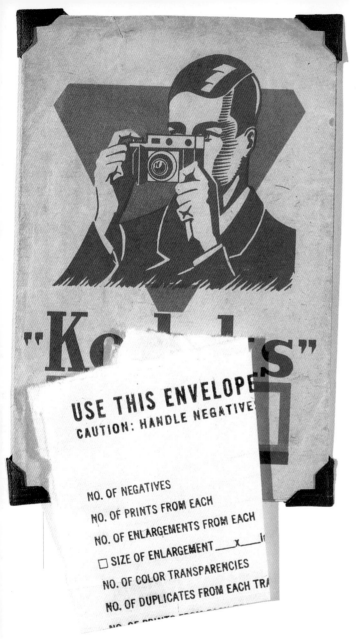

June 9:

I took in the negatives on the seventh to have small prints made and picked them up earlier today. Fifty prints—the 30 to go to those promised, some of her and her hand, and some of the places we visited. I held my breath when I came to the photos of her hand, but there truly is no sign of a pattern on her hand. But I'm back off to the photo lab to get larger prints just in case. It's too bad there are no photos of "Layesh." I could have sent them to his family to see if they could see a resemblance.

June 10:

I realized last night that I've been so caught up with visits and photos and organizing the next steps that I hadn't properly unpacked anything. Including the camera, which, it turns out, has a forgotten roll of film in it. So I went back to the lab again, picked up the enlargements and dropped off this last roll of film. Maybe they'll start giving me bulk discounts.

The enlargements again show an unmarked left hand. Yet she took very careful photographs of the hand and in one case must have had someone help her. I borrowed a magnifying glass at the film lab to see if there was any trace at all. I asked the technician to look at the negatives to see if there was anything that was too faint to print. He couldn't see anything. What on earth was she seeing?

later:
Just got back from a visit with her parents. Showed them the prints, trying to keep them involved. It's tempting to just keep on sorting through this without their endless questions. They just looked at the prints and said, "Another hand, what's this about? Why all of these hands?" They forget, it appears, that the hand was so pivotal to her disappearance. If only she had sketched the map as it appeared to her, maybe that would be a clue to what was going on in her mind.

June 11:
Terrible night last night. Couldn't sleep. Just kept going back over and over those weeks in Morocco. I drifted in and out of sleep for hours, walking down narrow streets in endless souks, squeezed between crowds of people, filled with the grinning faces from Lydia's photographs. I could see over the tops of everybody's head. I didn't watch where I was stepping or feel concerned that I might bump into someone. I just watched the distance, expecting to see

Lydia carried along by the throng. Now and then people would turn to me and ask me when I was going to send their photographs. When I looked at them, their faces would turn into Lydia's and then fade out of sight. Other times people would stick their hands in my face, and at one point an old man cupped his fetid hand over my mouth and waved the other one in front of my eyes. "*This is what a map looks like!*" he screamed at me. I couldn't see anything, I just struggled to remove his hand from my mouth. I tried to snap myself out of the dream, but the preoccupation with the photos and with Lydia has imprisoned my mind. I can remember telling myself to stop, but I'd start right back at the beginning, walking down the streets, crushed by the people, looking for Lydia.

noon:
Got the last contact sheet back. Photos of the Djemaa el Fna, the waiter at the café overlooking the square, some tourists snoozing in the shade of the café awning, books on a café table. She managed to photograph her arm. It must be just before she disappeared. There just isn't anything there. No matter how much I wish it there, it's not. Nothing. I'm so tired.

June 12:
I've been reading and rereading the journal, sticking photos in here and there where there's a gap. Looking at the contact sheets over and over. Back to my new home—the photo lab—to get

prints made of the last batch of negatives. Speaking of new homes, I'm going to try staying at Lydia's for a few nights. I can't go back to my apartment just yet, not after that dream.

I searched page by page through the guide book she found in the Tangier hotel, the *Guide Bleu.* There was a note in it—from her? It was stuck in among the folds of a map of Fes that had the Blvd du Quatrième Tirailleurs circled.

How sure she was that we were going to Morocco. I didn't have any such expectation. By the time we bought the ferry tickets to Tangier, I was convinced, but initially, as far as I was concerned, even up to

Algeciras, we could have gone in any of a number of other directions—Portugal, back up through Spain, along the coast to France, to the Canary Islands. It appears that she had this trip under far more control than I.

Another page from the *Guide Bleu* has time-tables for trains from city to city and certain train departures from Marrakech to Fes have been underlined in ballpoint pen. If she did this, what use would it be?—it's 1943.

June 13:
Had lunch with a possible new client. He's asking me if I'm planning to go back to North Africa some time soon. During lunch I wrote out a buy-sheet for him a page long so there may be a good enough reason to go back.

   Then went to the library and checked out a couple of history books on Morocco. When was the last time I read history? Makes me laugh—university. When was the last time I *willingly* read it. Try never.

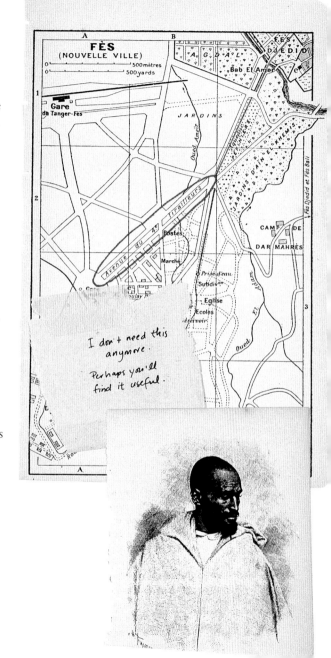

ROLL #5 - FORBES MUSEUM GARDEN

June 14:
Picked up the photos this morning. More hands, just hands—no maps, of course. I am wasting my time taking this crazy woman seriously.

later:
My days seem kind of useless. Now I'm *reading*, for God's sake. I don't know what use knowing chronologies of sultans is going to be to me.

June 16:
Have read nonstop since last journal entry. Finished the two histories, also a traveler's tale that I picked up yesterday. At least I've started to find it interesting. Seems that the three books have almost exhausted the local library's selection of decent-looking books on North Africa. Lydia's brother suggested the university library. I remember that she was always taking books out from there.

June 17:
Just got back from the campus library. What a dump! Can't even walk down the aisles without bumping your head on the humming, flickering fluorescent lights hanging from the low, low ceilings. And the library card—they made me pay $95 for a non-student card! And that's only good until September. Stayed in the building for just half an hour before I got the sneezes and a

headache. But have taken out a few more books at any rate, some more travelers' anecdotes and a couple of books about Moorish architecture.

June 18:

Had dinner last night with Lydia's mother and father. They wanted to know what I am planning to do, if I'm going back. But there isn't any sense going unless I hear something specific. Lydia's father has phoned the consulate in Rabat numerous times to complain that no one has done anything; I think they are probably working harder than I am to convince him that there's no need to go there. He doesn't seem to realize that I am just as upset as he about being useless. Part of it is just not knowing what one can do in a situation like this. The authorities assure us that we can do nothing but wait, that there is no point in carrying out our own searches. Does everyone who loses someone go through this sitting and waiting? Sometimes I think, the chance that she is alive aside, it would almost be better if she had died; then the rest of us would be free, not chained to her as we are now.

This was the first opportunity I had to show them all of her photographs, so between having dinner, arguing about not going back to Morocco, and going over the pictures, I was over there quite awhile. I didn't get prints from every shot, and lots of prints I've already sent away, but there were still a lot to go through. This is also the first time I've had to try to identify where each of the shots was taken. I'm afraid I failed miserably but no one really noticed. I could have made up anything and who would have been the wiser? However, for the first time, I felt as though I should take the photographs seriously and I was anxious to correctly identify each one. I would wince when I couldn't remember where a particular photo was taken, almost as if I could sense Lydia's disappointment that I hadn't been paying attention yet again.

June 19:
Was back at the library this morning returning the books I had finished and taking out a rather large stack of new ones. The library is starting to grow on me. For one thing, the smell of the books really takes me back to another time in spite of the dust and sneezing, and even though the shelves of books are squeezed tightly together with hardly enough room to allow a person to pass, well, there's rarely a soul in the sections that I'm interested in so it doesn't really matter. There's a compelling isolation in the library aisles that suits me fine right now. I can let my mind wander a bit and imagine Lydia sitting on the same linoleum floor, flipping through the same books, listening to the same squeak of library cart wheels from distant corners of the building. I can see her propping her feet on the lower shelves and leaning back against the spines of heavy encyclopedias, and above all I can see her cocking her head in order to

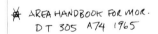

FEZ - FROM THE DOOR
OF THE MEDERSA
BOU INANIA, I THINK
ROLL 18

✱ AREA HANDBOOK FOR MOR.
DT 305 A74 1965

▣ RABINOW, PAUL

• GRAPAN ZANO, VINCENT
T U H A M I : PORTRAIT OF
A MOROCAN
GN 649 M65 C7 1980

STAIRS AT THE EXCELSIOR - FROM THE LANDING
ON THE FIRST FLOOR ⟹ ROLL # 25

pick out the muttered words of a reader a short distance away. Every once in a while someone walks by the aisle that I'm sheltered in. But I never realize until they are just past and if I glance up I get only a glimpse, if I see anything at all. The air moves, footsteps echo, a pencil clatters to the floor. I get a queer sensation that I'm waiting in the library expressly for Lydia, and with every passing shadow I raise my head in order to see her, to call out to her, to say, "I'm over here. Take a look at what I've found."

Lydia spent so much time up here, and I couldn't understand why. It seems impossible that I had no idea that this is how she occupied herself. We didn't have a lot of activities in common, and we haven't lived together for a number of years. But, all the same, we did spend a considerable amount of time with each other. It's odd admitting that the only person I could ever travel with is a person I found I could never live with. I think that when we traveled together we shed many of the obstacles that normally kept us distant. My distaste for her junk collecting, her nose in the gutter, so to speak. Her discomfort with my sense of order and my priceless "things." We couldn't take

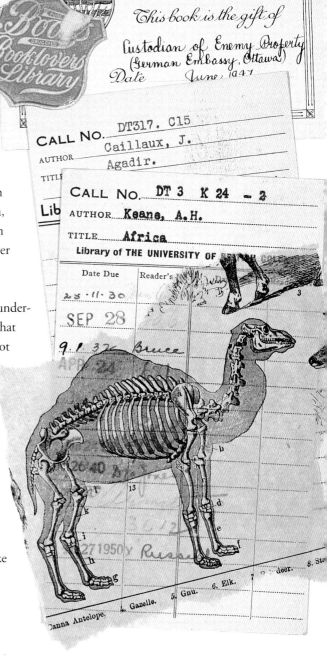

Canna Antelope. 4. Gazelle. 5. Gnu. 6. Elk. 7. deer. 8. St

STREET IN FES
OR, RATHER, DEAD-END
IN FES  ROLL #12

☐ WOOLMAN, DAVID
REBELS IN THE RIF
DT 324 W6 1968

◐ ABUN-NASR, J. M.
HISTORY OF THE MAGHREB
DT 194 A63 1971

△ UNIVERSAL GEOGRAPHER
-1ST FLOOR.

= GELLNER, ERNEST
MUSLIM SOCIETY
BP 163 G44 1981

these with us, could we? Only in our minds and even then only temporarily. Heavy burdens fall away so easily when one is traveling.

I wonder if she really knew anything about me, or if she considered that what there was to know about me was worthwhile.

At any rate, it was remarkable how I lost track of time today. Before I set off to the library, I checked through scraps of paper that Lydia had left around her apartment as well as the overdue book notices from the library. I went directly to the history section, which seemed to have grabbed her attention the most and where I had taken a couple of books out last time. History is mixed together with travelers' accounts, guide-books, geographical, economic, and social reports from days gone by, and business directories. The section is a ramshackle combination of Algeria, Morocco, and Tunisia. Without moving much further, I came across a huge section dealing with Egypt and then another for sub-Saharan Africa. Many of the books were from the 19th century and loaded with delicate engravings protected with slipsheets of vellum. The edges of the pages were brittle and yellow. It seems that anyone who opens these books now must, by the mere act of handling them, make an indelible mark. Some of the volumes had never been taken out. I set aside a couple of those just so I could be the first.

I opened a number of books labelled with book plates. The names and designs were a pleasurable reminder that these books were once cherished belongings of people, that they weren't always just neglected and collecting dust.

I double-checked the due date stamps and set aside the books that coincided with Lydia's reading lists. After gathering a pile of twenty or so I took them to one of the tables and sat down to quite a search.

The library was dead quiet. No one else in the history of North Africa section. When I looked at my watch, I was surprised to find that 5 hours had passed. Lydia had described her tattoo as a map with specific geographical features. There's no way I can patch that together without seeing what she saw, but she also mentioned eyes and hands. She wrote that she supposed they were charms against evil—I guess she picked that up from her reading. I've just been reading about this stuff, too. Kind of spooky. Judging from some

☐ - LANDAU, ROM
MOROCCO: MARRAKESH,
FEZ, RABAT
NK 1270 L3 1967

✡ — KASBAS OF SOUTH.
MOROCCO
DT 310.2 L3 1969

● — LEO AFRICANUS
HISTORY AND DESCRIP.
OF AFRICA.
NOT IN CATALOGUE.

■ GELLNER, ERNEST
SAINTS OF THE
ATLAS

• WESTERMARCK, E.
RITUAL & BELIEF
PN ?

• CROUTIER, ALEV L.
HAREM: THE WORLD
BEHIND THE VEIL
HQ 1170 C84 1989

STREET IN
MARRAKECH SOUK
(SUQ)? MARKET.
ROLL # 28 - UNMARKED

الحمد لله اشترى الحاج قريب عبد الله بربوسه البنتو وموح الرابع له
أخوهم ابراهيم بن تيشر ابشتنو ابشتنو ما بقا جميع الحمالة المستعملة للنقل
بهذا الموضع الذكر كذا بنفر ... شوارع ابشتنو والمحورة اعلاها السفير
وملك ورثة بني عمرا بنا دار الجملة واسماله الشجر بن السبيل لحسن بني
ملهت وفدلة المشتري وغرويلي الحمد بن بشير بجميع مبانها وما بعد وما وقع وكل
حقوقه كلوا الواخلة فيها والخارج منزعنها اشترى جميع انا ما للنفرط وميمورا
تقبيا وللاخيار بنفر فع رف مفعه ... أوان داراجع ولين مسكنا نار رقبته فيقبض البائع
المذكور من بربا المشتري المؤكور جميع الثمن المؤكور علينه وابر، ارحبيه وبرم
وتملك المشتري المؤكور شنترا، المؤكور ذكذا انا ما علا السعنه، وذلك والجميع
بادورا وبمو التقليب والرضا كاتجب وطربسه بهذا الجميع علا البا ابع المؤكور
وحد ذ الباربع ملادون الملك الصحيح ، و ملكه عن قدرة شرويه عليبر جال
كذلك ١٢ شهاد، وعزوكبه العشر بربن ى فى الفعر، علا ستة وعشرين وماتين
والمفع

accounts, a person in Morocco, at least in the past, couldn't move without security against wickedness or against the evil eye. Women and children, especially, were tattooed with hand or eye symbols, and doorways and walls of new buildings were stamped with the impressions of hands dipped in paint or mud. Lydia has a photo of such a wall somewhere in that batch.

June 20:

Going back to the library again today after I do some chores. Something I noticed yesterday: a number of books have interesting bits of paper left in them. One directory I looked through, Casablanca 1928, had a business card inserted into it. I'm beginning to see the attraction that Lydia had to picking up things like this. I was really tempted to keep it but put it back where I found it. I wrote down the name of the book, though, so I could have another look at it. It's tantalizing to consider actually taking stuff like that and saving it. But that would be like removing a page from the book. After all this time, it is part of the book's history, a record of who has looked in it before. But still . . . look at me arguing out such a dilemma in a journal.

HANDS ON THE WALL
CHECK ROLL #

BOWLES, PAUL —
· TOO FAR FROM HOME
  PS 3503 O86 1993
· UNWELCOME WORDS
  PS 3503 ..
· FIVE EYES - BY
  ABDESLAM BOULAICH
  PJ 8296 F44

FROM ROLL #28 - UNMARKED. A MEDERSA?
MEDERSA BEN YOUSSEF?

later:

Hauled an armload of books back home. I'm back in my own apartment—the bad nights have disappeared. The books weren't all from one section; I had to go from history to literature, from geography to linguistics, and on and on. I've tried starting with the books that were withdrawn around March, hoping that these are the ones she read. But they seem to have lost some of their magic in my apartment. I find I don't have the same compulsion to read them here. Perhaps there are too many other distractions. I'll take these back tomorrow and try working there again.

June 21:

Have spent the day so far in languages and found an Arabic/English dictionary published in 1918, with a page torn out of it. I know for a fact that Lydia had taken this book out. She had to pay a $2 fine on it at the end of March. I doubt very much that she tore the page out of it—she accumulates but is not destructive. It was a page starting out with words beginning with the Arabic letter for h. This is the only copy listed in the library catalogue, and it looks like a pretty rare book to me. Soft leather cover and coming apart at the spine. The edges of the pages are tinted with a

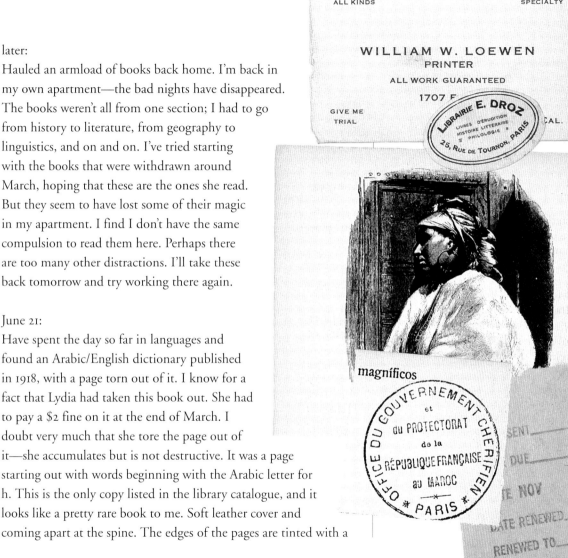

STREET IN TANGIER — ROLL #2 —OLD CITY NEAR HOTEL.

metallic ink and the paper is a fine onion skin. Such a beautiful book. The missing page is all the more enticing because of the beauty. Another dictionary will fill in the missing words I'm sure.

later:
Got sidelined going through the other Arabic dictionaries—all of them have been struck by the same destructive person and the same set of words is missing in each, words starting with h (or *ha* as I've discovered). I'll check at the bookstore—they must have Arabic/English dictionaries there. Have also started going page by page through a number of travelers' accounts for Morocco and North Africa. This is slow going because I keep getting caught up reading the books, which are surprisingly interesting. I've almost gone through the pile I had originally brought home. I've got pages of notes, lists copied from bibliographies, and potential readings on other subjects like folklore and fiction. And I now have a small envelope to tuck away any scraps of paper I find among the pages, which I justify by writing down the name of the book and the page number where they are found.

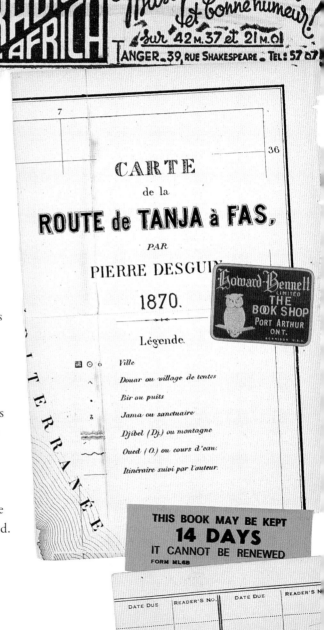

7
36

CARTE
de la
ROUTE de TANJA à FAS,
PAR
PIERRE DESGUI
1870.

Légende.

Ville
Douar ou village de tentes
Bir ou puits
Jama ou sanctuaire
Djibel (Dj.) ou montagne
Oued (O.) ou cours d'eau
Itinéraire suivi par l'auteur.

DATE DUE | READER'S NO. | DATE DUE | READER'S N

| أَلِف | 'alif | ا |
|---|---|---|
| بَا: | Bā' | ب |
| تَا: | Tā' | ت |
| ثَا: | Thā' | ث |
| جِيم | Jīm | ج |
| خَا: | Hā' | ح |
| خَا: | Khā' | خ |
| دَال | Dāl | د |
| ذَال | Dhāl | ذ |
| رَا: | Rā' | ر |
| زَاي | Zāy | ز |
| سِين | Sīn | س |
| شِين | Shīn | ش |
| صَاد | Ṣād | ص |
| ضَاد | Ḍād | ض |
| طَا: | Ṭā' | ط |
| ظَا: | Ẓā' | ظ |
| عَين | ʿayn | ع |
| غَين | Ghayn | غ |
| فَا: | Fā' | ف |
| قَاف | Qāf | ق |
| كَاف | Kāf | ك |
| لاَم | Lām | ل |
| مِيم | Mīm | م |
| نُون | Nūn | ن |
| هَا: | Hā' | ه |
| وَاو | Wāw | و |
| يَا: | Yā' | ي ى |
| هَمْزَة | Hamza | ء |

This way I can return them when I am sure that there is no further need for them. I feel kind of badly about this, but they've become an obsession and I really can't help myself.

I still don't understand why I feel so comfortable in this bunker of a library. The top of my head grazes the fluorescent tubes when I stand up straight. The light is so bad that in some of the aisles it's quite dark even at noon. I have paper cuts on my fingers from flipping past so many pages, and my nose twitches continuously from the dust. And I haven't achieved a thing.

June 22:
Had to stay home today to meet some clients, although the idea of going off buying again is distinctly unappealing. These clients think I'm pretty resourceful, of course. They don't know that much of that came from Lydia. I don't think she knew it. But I have to consider the future. If I don't continue doing this, what would I do? Get a real job? Ha. Of course, I could always sell off some of my collection.

later:
The hair on my neck is standing on end. I have found an account by a man who traveled through Fes in the early '40s. He related a story of meeting a Muslim, a café owner, who had just returned from Mecca. This man told the traveler that soon after he arrived in Mecca, he noticed that he had been mysteriously tattooed on his arm and that, after much thought, he interpreted the tattoo as

the story of his life. The pattern of the tattoo was, according to the writer, in the form of a map, beginning at the wrist and climbing up the arm. The café owner had, the writer continued, told no one in his family that this map had appeared of its own accord. He told them that he had done it while he was away. To them this was shameful enough.

The traveler was clearly impressed with this story; it occupied several pages of his account of Fes and ended with an account of the Moroccan's plans to leave Fes and follow the map. For by that point the map had grown beyond his life and had begun to show a new future. The nameless café owner took pains, according to the writer, to insist that this had nothing to do with his religion; he was a devout Muslim, but he was also a man of the world. He was not searching for any meaning to his life—with his family and his café and his friends, his life was as complete as any. But it had to do with his insatiable desire to see the world. And anyone who had such a desire had to know which way to go. Those lucky enough to have the way pointed out to them would have to follow the route or lose the chance forever.

SHORT-TRIP GUIDE.

306

TRAV.—*Pas si vite!* or, *Allez plus doucement!* (Pro. Pah se veet; or allay ploo doosmong. Eng. Go more slowly.)

TRAV. (When getting out of the cab, to have it wait)—*Attendez moi ici; je vais revenir; or, je reviens dans quelque minutes.* (Pro. Je vay rayvaneer; or, je rayveeon dawn kelk meenwheet. Eng. Wait for me here I will return; or, I will return in a few minutes.)

CABMAN.—*Mon argent, Monsieur!* (Pro. Mong arjong, Mossiew! Eng. My money, sir!)

TRAV.—*Voici.* (Pro. Vwassee. Eng. Here it is.)

CABMAN.—*Plus encore le pour boire, Monsieur!* (Pro. Ploo sancoar leh poor bwar, Mossiew! Eng. More yet, sir: the drink-money!)

TRAV.—*Combien de pour boire?* (Pro. Combeyon deh poor bwar? Eng. How much drink-money?)

TRAV.—*Ce n'est pas possible de payer rien de plus.* (Pro. Ce nay pah poseebl deh paya reeon deh ploo. Eng. It is not possible [for me] to pay any thing more.)

TRAV.—*Arrêtez!* or, *arrêtez vous, cocher!* (Pro. arraytay; or, arraytay vous, coshay. Eng. Stop! or, stop, conchman.)

**Eating and Drinking.**

ORDERS TO WAITERS.—*Garçon, faites moi servir.* (Pro. Gahsoon, fayt mwa sareveer. Eng. Walter, attend on me.) *Je désire dîner.* (Pro. Je deseer deenay. Eng. I wish dinner.) *Donnez moi du potage à la Julienne.* (Pro. Donnay mwa deuh potahj ah lah Jzhulion. Eng. Give me some soup a la Julienne.) *Du rosbif bien cuit.* (Pro. Deuh roosbif beeyon quee. Eng. Some roast-beef well done.) *Du rosbif saignant.* (Pro. Deuh roosbif sainyong. Eng. Some roast-beef rare.) *Du porc roti.* (Pro. Deuh pork roatee. Eng. Some roast pork.) *Du pain.* (Pro. Deuh pan. Eng. Some bread.) *Encore un peu plus de beurre.* (Pro. oon pew ploo deh burr. Eng. A little more butter.) *Une tasse deh caffay.* Eng. A cup of coffee.) *Un verre doe.* Eng. A glass of water.) *Un verre ... ... ... ... Eng. A glass of ice-water.)* ... Eng. Some potatoes.) deh van ruzjh. ... Eng. A ... ...lanc. (Pro. Oon daymee ; white wine.) *Apportez* oon awsyet pronpr. Eng. ...poulet. (Pro. Oon frecasa... ...ux côtelets de veau. (Pr... ...lets.) *Du mouton bouill...* ...oiled mutton.) *Deux ou...* ...boiled eggs.) *Du poisso...* Eng. Boiled fish.) *Du p...* ...deh pwassong boolee. Eng. Some cake.) *Du pâte...* au sucre. (Pro. Deuh pan o sukr. ...

Br... deh poo... Deuh cotaylay de vo... (Pro. Deuh mootong boolee. Eng... frits. (Pro. Deuz ufe freet, ... todilli. (Pro. Deuh pwassong boolee. ...

DISCARD

I sat rereading the entry for some time. It seemed to resemble the little Lydia wrote about her conversation with Layesh. And then I scrambled over to the folder holding the photos and looked through the pictures of Lydia's arm: there is a map on her arm in each photograph. Why can I see it now? I'm actually frightened. Has something happened to the photographs, or to me?

The map clearly starts at the wrist and climbs up the arm to the elbow. She kept this from me the whole time and I didn't notice a thing, and yet would I have been able to see it if she had tried to show me? Was she really waiting for me to say something? I know she was. She mentioned in the journal that any comment would have sufficed. And then when I didn't say anything, she gave me up? No, too petty. Was she afraid I would belittle her when this was obviously so important? I can't deny that I might have treated it lightly. She clearly didn't realize that I wouldn't be able to see it, that probably no one could see it except her—and Layesh. It's as if part of her were traveling during a different time, on a different trip.

But this doesn't explain why she chose to keep the existence of the tattoo a mystery to me. I know she wrote about it in the journal, I know she photographed it, but she knew I had no interest in reading the journal and she wasn't so naïve as to expect that I would change my mind. I have been under the illusion that her journal entries were attempts to create a new reality, one far more interesting than that which our lives had provided. And now I find that while hers was spiraling beyond control I was digging myself deeper into my blissfully mundane fog. How did she put it in the

early days of the trip? "We walk towards nowhere, one foot in front of the other." Or something like that. No wonder she disappeared. I was clearly not capable of coping with her situation. She's probably better off on her own than with me. It's taken a lot for me to realize this, and perhaps now I *will* be able to understand. But I must first ask the question, why her? These things don't happen to ordinary people like us, people without superstitions. But is what happened supernatural or grounded firmly on earth? Perhaps she had a goal on this trip that I was unaware of and the tattoo was a natural result of pursuing this goal.

I can't take my eyes off of the last photograph. The tattoo is so beautiful, so compelling, but I understand why Lydia wrote of a powerful sense of revulsion. I can't imagine how I would have reacted had it happened to me.

I believe I now must return to Morocco. I want to return to Morocco.

ESPAGNE

GIBRALTAR

Détroit de Gibraltar

MER

C.<sup>en</sup> C. Spartel

Malabat

CEUTA

MÉDITERRANÉE

R. de Jouania

TANJA

Suani

TÉTOUAN

Habin

ER - RIF

Petit

Atlas

35

O. El Kous

OUAZZY

Sidi Meymoun

Dj. Werza

Dj. Klikkha

OULED ESSA

34

Mehedia

Rabat

Feza

Theza

R. Tensift

M A R O C

B. Werza

O. Sbou

FAS

34

32

6                    4   West of

Am. Photo-Lithographic Co. N.Y. (Osborne's Process)

# DISCOVERY AND ADVENTURE

## IN

# AFRICA.

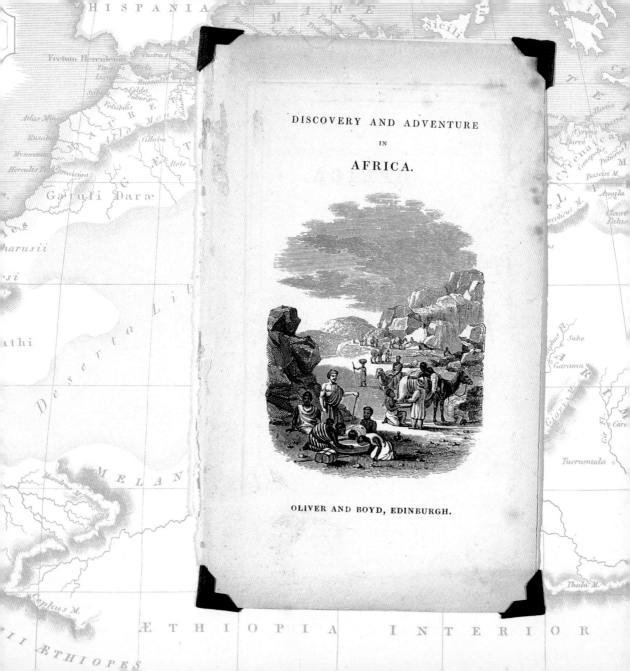

OLIVER AND BOYD, EDINBURGH.

July 3, the plane:
Following the same route, except I'll fly directly to Tangier from London instead of going overland. Sure would have been cheaper just to have stayed there in the first place.

July 5, Tangier:
I'm in the same hotel at the Petit Socco in the medina. The hotel owner doesn't recognize me, or if he does he hasn't asked about Lydia. What did Lydia say his first name was? Can't remember.

I'll stay here overnight and catch the train to Fes tomorrow. I don't know why Fes, except that's where Lydia met Layesh, and Layesh must be the means by which I'll find her.

later:
Asked the proprietor of the hotel if I could look through the guest registry to check the date when we stayed here last. Ahmed, that's his name. He opened up a large cupboard behind where he was sitting, and I saw a number of ledgers in addition to the one he pulled out for me. So I asked him if I could look back through past years. He misunderstood me, pointed to the one he had originally given me, and turned his back in a display of absolute indifference. Normally, I would give up. No, normally, I wouldn't even ask such a thing. This is all haywire—I persisted, muttering any French I could muster, even if it didn't make sense. He eventually turned around and looked at me for a second or two, with no expression on his face, I might add. I remember him talking to

3RD
DPT: 5:45 PM
    FLT 897
ARR: LDN HEATHROW
     10:45 AM - 4TH

4TH
DPT: 3:15 PM
ARR: TANGIER
     6:20 PM
     FLT 1120

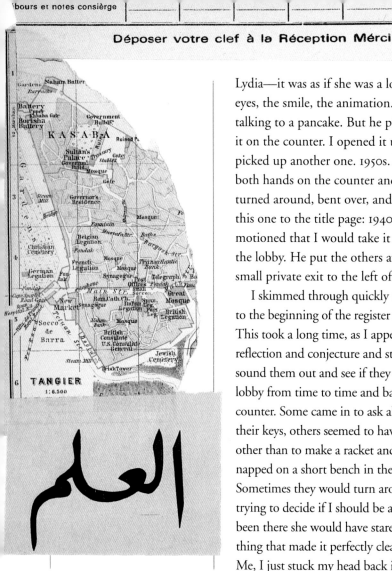

Lydia—it was as if she was a long-lost sister, the warmth in his eyes, the smile, the animation. To me, he might as well have been talking to a pancake. But he picked up another journal and flung it on the counter. I opened it up. 1960s. I shook my head. He picked up another one. 1950s. I shook my head again. He put both hands on the counter and looked at me again. Then he turned around, bent over, and picked up the next one. I opened this one to the title page: 1940s. I nodded gratefully at him and motioned that I would take it over to one of the chairs that lined the lobby. He put the others away and left the lobby by way of a small private exit to the left of the counter.

I skimmed through quickly at first, but finding nothing, returned to the beginning of the register and went through each of the entries. This took a long time, as I appear to have picked up the habit of reflection and conjecture and stopped at a number of the names to sound them out and see if they were familiar. People came into the lobby from time to time and banged on the bell at the reception counter. Some came in to ask about rooms, others came in to get their keys, others seemed to have no other purpose for coming in other than to make a racket and wake the proprietor up (he cat-napped on a short bench in the little room behind the counter). Sometimes they would turn around and study me for a minute, as if trying to decide if I should be approached to help them. If Lydia had been there she would have stared straight at them and said something that made it perfectly clear that conversation was welcome. Me, I just stuck my head back in my book, my perfect barrier.

| Date | Nom et Adresse | N° | Chambre | Depart |
|------|----------------|-----|---------|--------|
| 6 avril 1943 | B. F. Baldrati, Paris VII | 10096 | 21 | 12 avril |
| 6 avril | Camille Aymard, Montreuil s/Bois 00578 | | 12 et 14 | 7 avril |
| 6 avril | Leon Steinville et famille, Marseille | 11427 | 16 | 24 avril |
| 6 avril | FARJALLAH HAIK, MARRAKECH | ~ | 24 | 8 avril |
| 6 avril | Carlos d'Ogulla, Sevilla, Esp | e847 | # 9 | 9 avril |
| 6 avril | Marius Richard, 15 bis rue Richard Lenoir Paris | 19820 | 10 | 7 avril |
| 6 avril | Louis Chauvet, Casablanca | 09438 | 22 | 8 avril |
| 6 avril | M. L. Geunis 25 rue de Passy | 89 09380 | 32 | 8 avril |
| 6 avril | Mlle Marie Guyon, à Assac, par Valence | 16894 | 34 | 2 mai |
| 6 | ... en 6 avenue Balfourier XVI | 18632 | 15 | 9 avril |
| 5 avril | Walter Martin, Isabel Martin, ... von Fidelstr Wien | 14781 | 18 | 10 avril |
| 8 avril | ... | 12354 | 22 | 10 mai |
| 9 avril | M. Rambaud Roger d'Albigeois, London | E65094 | 19 | ... avril |
| 9 avril | Madame Jeanne Macler Kervozes | | 24 | 10 avril |
| 9 avril | BOUFOUS Said, CASABLANCA | 10875 | 22 | 12 avril |
| 9 avril | Oberveneau, 22 rue des Regards, Paris | 1764 | 29 | 18 avril |
| 9 avril | Lydia Usher, Canada | ~ | | 13 avril |
| 9 avril | Yosef Touraines, Marseilles France | 07653 | 15 | 11 avril |
| 9 avril | A. Kuhlmann, Sulzbach | AP60472 | 28 | 13 avril |
| 9 avril | Fernand, Remeine, Tetouan | 15554 | 14 | 10 avril |
| 10 avril | R. C. Beaubrun, Fontevrault | DD68727-83 | 38 | 24 avril |
| | Alphonse Metween, Toulouse (et famille) | ~ | | |
| | | 18725 | 17 | 22 avril |
| | | | | 22 avril |

I don't think I knew what I was looking for, but I found it. In 1943 there was an entry for April 9, signed by Lydia, in her handwriting. The ink was faded as though she had really signed it then. She had been given room 14, the same room we had together three months ago. I put the register back on the counter and reached over to the desk behind in order to get the current book. The proprietor was still snoozing and I definitely didn't want to disturb him again. I opened up the ledger to April 9 of this year and found only my name listed even though I know we both registered. I ripped the page out of the old book; nobody will ever miss it.

Some people came in at this point so I closed the book, stuffed the paper in my pocket, and stood aside for them, motioning that the proprietor was behind the curtains. They rang the bell and waited for him to get up and come out front. After he finished dealing with them, I asked him if room 14 was free. He said something to me in French, probably something to do with people not being content or people causing too much trouble, but the room was free so we somehow negotiated a room change for me. I took the new key and moved my things from the room on the second floor back down to the first floor.

I opened up the door to a completely different room than the one we had stayed in. I'm in here now. The floor plan is the same, but it's been furnished with brand-new furniture; when we stayed here before everything was clean but shabby. The tiles have been replaced; they no longer shift in place as I walk about. The curtains aren't in shreds, the taps don't drip, the doors and windows shut properly. I pulled back the covers, remembering Lydia's observation about the sheets. The sheets are still too short for the bed, but they are new or newish, no cigarette burns, no evidence of mending.

I write this as though I have accepted the odd things that I am starting to observe around me. But something that I can't accept: for a lark I opened up the drawers of the freshly painted wardrobe in the corner and inside the drawer was a *Guide Bleu*, a *Guide Bleu* from 1943. I rushed over to my suitcase and threw everything out, searching for Lydia's *Guide Bleu*, which I had brought with me. It was no longer in my bag. Someone had taken it out and placed it here, for this is the same one.

Evening:
I'm in a café, one of the many that Lydia and I sat in for endless hours when we first arrived in Tangier, and I see the man who had stared at her so openly, the man who looks like Layesh. She had pointed him out here and at other cafés as well. Damned if he isn't watching me. God, I wish I smoked. I mortify myself sometimes. I came back to Morocco to find Lydia and he is the means, but I'm paralyzed. I can't move.

July 6:
I've woken up with flea bites on my left hand, just like Lydia.

later:
I'm sitting on the terrace at the restaurant just down the street from the hotel having break-fast and the man who looks like Layesh is here again. I'm going to try staring back at him.

Later, train to Fes:
Well, when I looked at the man in the café he got up from his table and came over to mine. I asked him to sit down. I can't believe I did that—I actually asked him to sit down at my table and he did.

He formally introduced himself although I know we both realized there was no need. He told me, in a cold, hard voice that his name was Layesh Boussalem, and he said he had been waiting for me with a message from Lydia. With that he yanked the sleeve of his shirt up to his elbow with a force that ripped off the button of the cuff. There, exposed on his tightly-muscled arm, was a tattoo, similar to the one in Lydia's photos, but more extensive, more complicated, more worn.

My face burned, my eyes burned. I couldn't stand to look at him or his arm. I didn't trust myself to break the silence. He then pulled his sleeve back over his arm and spoke to me quietly as I stared at the ground. With his right hand methodically and repetitively smoothing the sleeve, he described Lydia's reluctance to get in touch with me again until she discovered that I'd returned to Morocco. I became overwhelmed first with a sadness and then a relief that brought on shaming but uncontrollable tears which I wiped away with the back of my hand. He talked on, his voice embracing me with hazy phrases that made no sense, that ran together weaving a story of arrival and departure, of direction and disorientation, of past and present. The words curled around my neck and caressed the lobes of my ears. I tried to brush them away with my hands, as if they were a nuisance, but found myself paralyzed both by his soft breath which, as aromatic as camphor, had the powerful force of a strong wind and by the vision of his arm which I couldn't shake.

At one point I thought Lydia was sitting at the table with us, staring at me as directly as he. But Lydia wasn't there, just him and his persistent, soft, compelling voice telling and retelling Lydia's message. I got up from the table in the midst of the narrative and the words followed me back to the hotel, they whispered in my ear as I packed my bags, they wound about my head like a tight band while I checked out and walked to the station.

I'm sitting here, on this train to Fes, grateful to be alone in the carriage with this voice of Layesh's and these words of Lydia's. For what I have to hide from the world is something that I must show to Lydia. Here, amidst the blurred vision of passing scenery, the warm, leathery smell of the upholstery, the prickle of dust in the nostrils, is my reason for returning to Morocco—hesitant, fine, red and blue lines of rivers and roads on my arm. The marks of an eternal traveler, the passport back to Lydia.

# CARTE
### DU
## VERSANT OCCIDENTAL
### DU
# MAROC
## (MOGHREB-EL-AKSA)
### par
### PIERRE DESGUIN.

### LÉGENDE.

Terrain quaternaire et moderne
— pliocène.
— miocène.
— éocène.
— crétacé    supérieur
          inférieur.
— jurassique.
Argilite calcarifère
Poudingue ferrugineux
Terrain plutonien.

MOROCCO

Gibraltar
Tar
Ceuta (Span.)
talaya
Tetuan (Span.)
Vigia
Anna
Fogaaza
Fez
Sofero
Tessa

a
p
m
e
C2
C1
J
ac
pf
i

# L'AFRIQUE
## D'APRÈS LES VOYAGEURS LES PLUS CÉLÈBRES
### Par un homme de lettres.
#### DEUXIÈME ÉDITION.

# LILLE
## L. LEFORT, IMPRIMEUR-LIBRAIRE
### 1852

DAR BEIDA
(Casablanca)

Omm-er-Rbia
C. Mazagan
AZIMOUR
DIDA (Mazagan)